PETER ABÉLARD

PETER ABÉLARD

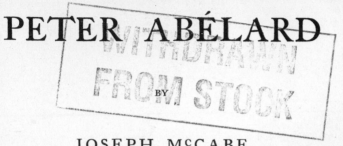

BY

JOSEPH McCABE

AUTHOR OF

'TWELVE YEARS IN A MONASTERY,' ETC.

DESORMAIS

LONDON

DUCKWORTH and CO.

3 HENRIETTA STREET, W.C.

1901

Edinburgh: T. and A. CONSTABLE, (late) Printers to Her Majesty

PREFACE

THE author does not think it necessary to offer any apology for having written a life of Abélard. The intense dramatic interest of his life is known from a number of brief notices and sketches, but English readers have no complete presentation of the facts of that remarkable career in our own tongue. The *History of Abailard* of Mr. Berington, dating from the eighteenth century, is no longer adequate or useful. Many French and German scholars have re-written Abélard's life in the light of recent knowledge and feeling, but, beyond the short sketches to be found in Compayré, Poole, Rashdall, Cotter Morison, and others, no English writer of the nineteenth century has given us a complete study of this unique and much misunderstood personality. Perhaps one who has also had a monastic, scholastic, and ecclesiastical experience may approach the task with a certain confidence.

In the matter of positive information the last century has added little directly to the story of Abélard's life. Indirectly, however, modern research has necessarily helped to complete the picture ; and modern feeling, modern humanism, reinterprets much of the story.

Since the work is intended for a circle of readers who cannot be assumed to have a previous acquaintance with the authorities who are cited here and there, it is necessary to indicate their several positions in advance. The chief sources of the story are the letters of Abélard and Heloise. The first letter of the series, entitled the 'Story of my Calamities,' is an autobiographical sketch, covering the first fifty years of Abélard's life. To these must be added the letters of St. Bernard, abbot of Clairvaux: of Peter the Venerable, abbot of Cluny: of Jean Roscelin, canon of Compiègne, Abélard's early teacher : and of Fulques of Deuil, a contemporary monk. A number of Latin works written shortly after Abélard's death complete, or complicate, the narrative. The principal of these are: the *Vita Beati Bernardi*, written by his monk-secretary :

the *Vita Beati Goswini*, by two monks of the period : the *De gestis Frederici I.* of a Cistercian bishop, Otto of Freising : the *Metalogicus* and the *Historia Pontificalis* of John of Salisbury : and the *Vita Ludovici Grossi* and *De rebus a se gestis* of Suger, abbot of St. Denis, and first royal councillor. Many of the chronicles of the twelfth century also contain brief references.

Chief amongst the later French historians is Du Boulai with his *Historia Universitatis Parisiensis*—'the most stupid man who ever wrote a valuable book,' says Mr. R. L. Poole. Amongst other French chroniclers of the sixteenth and seventeenth centuries we may mention: De Launoy (*De scholis celebrioribus*), Dubois (*Historia Ecclesiae Parisiensis*), Lobineau (*Histoire de Bretagne*), Félibien (*Histoire de l'abbaye de Saint Denys* and *Histoire de la ville de Paris*), Longueval (*Histoire de l'Eglise Gallicane*), Tarbé (*Recherches historiques sur la ville de Sens*), and, of course, the *Histoire littéraire de la France*, *Gallia Christiana*, and ecclesiastical historians generally.

A large number of 'lives' of Abélard have been founded on these documents. In French

we have *La vie de P. Abélard* of Gervaise, a
monkish admirer of the eighteenth century, far
from ascetic in temper, but much addicted to
imaginative description : the historical essay of
Mme. and M. Guizot, prefixed to M. Oddoul's
translation of the letters of Abélard and Heloise :
the *Abélard* of M. Rémusat, pronounced by Ste.
Beuve himself to be ' un chef d'œuvre ' : and the
Lettres Complètes of M. Gréard, with a helpful
introduction.   In German Reuter chiefly discusses
Abélard as a thinker in his *Geschichte der religiösen
Entklärung* : Deutsch is mainly pre-occupied with
his theology in his *Peter Abälard*, but gives an
exhaustive study of the last years of his life in
Abälard's Verurtheilung zu Sens : Neander discusses him in his *Heilige Bernhard* : and Hausrath
offers the most complete and authoritative study
of his career and character in his recent *Peter
Abälard*.   In English we have, as I said, the
eighteenth-century work of Berington, a small
fantastic American version (quite valueless), and
the more or less lengthy studies of Abélard found
in Rashdall's fine *Universities of Europe*, Cotter
Morison's *Life and Times of St. Bernard* (scarcely

a judicious sketch), Compayré's *Abélard and the Universities* (in which the biography is rather condensed), Roger Vaughan's *Life of St. Thomas of Aquin*, and Mr. R. L. Poole's *Illustrations of the History of Mediæval Thought* (from whom we may regret we have not received a complete study of Abélard).

January 31, 1901.

CONTENTS

CHAPTER I

THE QUEST OF MINERVA

PETER ABÉLARD was born towards the close of the eleventh century. No other personality that we may choose to study leads to so clear and true an insight into those strange days as does that of the luckless Breton philosopher. It was the time of transition from the darkest hour of mediæval Europe to a period of both moral and intellectual brilliance. The gloom of the 'century of iron' still lay on the land, but it was already touched with the faint, spreading dawn of a new idealism. There is, amongst historians, a speculation to the effect that the year 1000 of the Christian era marked a real and very definite stage in the history of thought. Usually we do violence to events by our chronological demarcations; but it is said that Christendom confidently expected the threatened rolling-up of the heavens and the earth to take place in the year 1000. Slowly, very slowly, the sun crept over the dial of the heavens before the eyes of idle men. But no Christ rode on the clouds, and no Anti-Christ came into the cities. And the heaviness was lifted from the breasts of men, and the blood danced merrily in their veins once more. They began again 'to feel the joy of existence,' as an old writer has it, and to build up their towers afresh in the sun-light.

It was a strangely chequered period, this that changed the darkness of the tenth into the comparative radiance of the thirteenth century. All life was overcast by densest ignorance and grossest lust and fiercest violence, the scarcely altered features of the 'converted' northern barbarians; yet the light of an ideal was breaking through, in the pure atmosphere of reformed monasteries, in the lives of saintly prelates and women refined beyond their age, and in the intellectual gospel of a small band of thinkers and teachers. Amid the general degradation of the Church and the cloister strong souls had arisen, ardent with a contagious fire of purity. High-minded prelates had somehow attained power, in spite of the net of simony and corruption. The sons of St. Benedict, rising and falling too often with the common tide, had, nevertheless, guarded some treasures of the earlier wisdom, and shared them lovingly at their gates with the wandering scholar. Thousands there were who could close heart and home at the fiery word of a preacher, and go to starve their souls in the living tomb of a monastery. Thousands could cast down their spades and their wine-cups, and rush to meet death in the trail of a frenzied hermit.[1] They were the days of the travail of the spirit ; and they rise before us in arresting vision when we look into the life of Peter Abélard.

That life begins some day in the last decade of the eleventh century, when the young Breton, then in his fifteenth or sixteenth year, went out from his father's castle into the bright world on the quest of Minerva. Of his earlier years we know nothing. Later fancy has brooded over them to some purpose, it is true, if there are any

[1] I am thinking, of course, of the thousands of simple folk who rushed blindfold into the fatal procession towards Jerusalem, setting their children on their rude carts, and asking naïvely, at each tower that came in sight in their own France, if that was the Holy City : those whose bones marked the path to Palestine for later Crusaders. As to the professional warriors, there is surely more humour than aught else in the picture of the King of France and his like setting forth to 'do penance' for their vice and violence by a few months of adventure, carnage, and pillage.

whom such things interest. The usual unusual events were observed before and after his birth, and the immortal swarm of bees that has come down the ages, kissing the infant lips of poets and philosophers, did not fail to appear at Pallet. In point of sober fact, we rely almost exclusively on Abélard's autobiography for the details of his earlier career, and he tells us nothing of his childhood, and not much of his youth. It matters little. The life of a soul begins when it looks beyond the thoughts of parents and teachers—if it ever do—out into the defiant world, and frames a view and a purpose.

The home from which Abélard issued, somewhere about the year 1095, was an ancient castle at Pallet, in Brittany, about eleven miles to the south-east of Nantes. At the end of the village, which was threaded on the high road from Nantes to Poitiers, a steep eminence dominated the narrow flood of the Sanguèze. The castle was built on this: overlooking the village more, as it chanced, in a spirit of friendly care than of haughty menace. The spot is still visited by many a pilgrim—not with a priestly benediction; but the castle is now the mere relic of a ruin. In the most penetrating movements of his prophetic genius, Abélard never foresaw the revolt of the serfs, or indeed any economic development. In this one respect he failed to detect and outstrip what little advance was made in his day. His father's castle has disappeared with the age it belonged to, and the sons of his vassals now lay the bones of their dead to rest on his desolated hearth.

Bérenger, the father, was a noble of a rare type. He had fortunately received a little culture before setting out in the service of Hoel IV., Duke of Brittany and Count of Nantes, and he in turn communicated his taste and his knowledge to his children. From the fact, too, that he and his wife Lucia adopted the monastic life a few years after Abélard's departure, we may gather that they were also above the moral level of their class. It is not idle to note that Abélard's mind encountered no evil or irreligious influences when it first opened. All the circumstances that are known to us suggest a gentle, uplifting, and reverential education. He was the eldest of the sons of Bérenger ; and, partly, no doubt, because greater care had been taken with his education, partly in the necessary consciousness of mental power, he early determined to leave home, and wander over the land in search of learning. His words give one the impression

that he shouldered a wallet, and sallied forth
alone, after the adventurous fashion of the day.
However that may be, he says that he resolved to
leave the chances of the favour of Mars to his
brothers, and set out to woo the gentler Minerva.
Abandoning the rights of primogeniture and the
possible grace of kings, he passed away from the
great castle, and turned eagerly in the direction
of the nearest school.

It was not uncommon in those 'Dark Ages'
for a young noble to resign the comfort of the
château and the glamour of a courtly life in this
way. The scholastic fever, which was soon to
inflame the youth of the whole of Europe, had
already set in. You could not travel far over
the rough roads of France without meeting some
foot-sore scholar, making for the nearest large
monastery or episcopal town. Before many years,
it is true, there was a change, as the keen-eyed
Jew watched the progress of the fever. There
arose an elaborate system of conveyance from
town to town, an organisation of messengers to
run between the château and the school, a smiling
group of banks and bankers. But in the earlier
days, and, to some extent, even later, the scholar
wandered afoot through the long provinces of

France. Here and there a noble or a wealthy merchant would fly past in his silks and furs, with a body-guard of a dozen stout fellows ; or a poor clerk would jog along on his ass, looking anxiously towards each wood or rock that bordered the road ahead. Robbers, frequently in the service of the lord of the land, infested every province. It was safest to don the coarse frieze tunic of the pilgrim, without pockets, sling your little wax tablets and style at your girdle, strap a wallet of bread and herbs and salt on your back, and laugh at the nervous folk who peeped out from their coaches over a hedge of pikes and daggers. Few monasteries refused a meal or a rough bed to the wandering scholar. Rarely was any fee exacted for the lesson given. For the rest, none were too proud to earn a few sous by sweeping, or drawing water, or amusing with a tune on the reed-flute : or to wear the cast-off tunics of their masters.

It is fitting that we should first find little Pierre —Master Roscelin recalls him in later years as ' the smallest of my pupils '—under the care of a rationalist scholar. Love was the first rock on which the fair promise of his early manhood was shattered, but throughout the long, sternly religious years that followed, it was his restless application of reason to the veiled dogmas of faith that brought endless cruelty and humiliation upon him. Now, Jean Roscelin, canon of Compiègne, was the rationalist of his day. As Abélard was fated to do, he had attempted to unveil the super-sacred doctrine of the Trinity; not in the spirit of irreverent conceit, with which people credited both him and Abélard, but for the help of those who were afflicted with a keen intellect and an honest heart. For this he had been banished from England in 1093, and from the kingdom of France, and had settled in one or other of the Gaulish provinces.

Mme. Guizot, in her very careful study of Abélard, sees no evidence for the statement that he studied under Roscelin, but the fact is now beyond dispute. Otto von Freising, a contemporary historian, says that he 'had Roscelin for his first master'; Aventinus and others also speak of Roscelin as an early teacher of his. Roscelin himself, in a letter which it seems 'frivolous,' as Deutsch says, to hesitate to accept, claims that Abélard sat at his feet—it was the literal practice in those days—'from boyhood to youth.' Abélard, on the other hand, writes that he attended Roscelin's lectures 'for a short time'; but this correspondence took place at a moment when the one would be greatly disposed to exaggerate and the other to attenuate. An anonymous anecdote, which we shall examine presently, pretends that he found Roscelin unsatisfactory, but 'controlled his feeling so far as to remain under Roscelin for a year.' It is clear enough that he spent a few of his earlier years on the hay-strewn floor of Master Roscelin's lecture-hall.

There is some uncertainty as to the locality, but a sufficient indication to impart an interest to the question. Roscelin says it was at the 'Locensis ecclesia.' This is easily understood if we interpret it to mean the monastery of Locmenach[1] in Brittany. The monks of St. Gildas, on the coast of Brittany, a wild band whose closer acquaintance we shall make later on, had established a branch monastery at Loc-menach. As will appear in due time, they would be likely to have small scruple about increasing its revenue by erecting a chair for one of the most famous dialecticians in Christendom, in spite of his condemnation for heresy at London and

[1] Locmenach = *locus monachorum*, 'the place of the monks.' The older name was Moriacum. It is now called Locminé, and lies a few miles to the east of Vannes.

Soissons. We have no special information about
the manner of school-life at Locmenach, save
that we know the monks of St. Gildas to have
been the living antithesis to the good monks of
Bec ; but it is interesting to find Abélard studying
dialectics under a famous rationalist, and in a
monastery that was subject to the Abbey of
St. Gildas of Rhuys. The dark pages of his
later history will give point to the dual circumstance.

There is one other, and less reliable, account of
Abélard in his school-days. In an anecdote which
is found in one or two older writers, and on the
margin of an old Abélard manuscript, it is stated
that he studied mathematics under a certain Master
Tirricus. The anecdote is generally rejected as
valueless, on the ground that it contains clear
trace of the work of a 'constructive imagination';
but Mr. Poole points out that 'there is no reason
to doubt' the authenticity of the substance of the
narrative, and it seems to me that the fictional
element may be reduced to a very slender quantity.
The story runs that Tirric, or Theodoric, one day
found Abélard shedding tears of fruitless per-
spiration over mathematical problems. He had
already, it is said, mastered the higher branches

of knowledge, and was even teaching, but had omitted mathematics, and was endeavouring to remedy the omission by taking private lessons from Tirric. Noting his effort, the master is represented to say: 'What more can the sated dog do than lick the bacon?' 'To lick the bacon' is, in the crude Latinity of the age, *bajare lardum*, and the story pretends the phrase afforded a nickname for Pierre (Bajolard or Baiolard), and was eventually rounded into Abélard or Abailard. The construction is so crude, and the probability that Abélard is a surname needing no legendary interpretation is so high, that the whole anecdote is often contemptuously rejected. It is surely much more reasonable to read the phrase as a pun on Abélard's name, which some later writer, to whom the name was unfamiliar, has taken in a constructive sense.[1]

There are several good reasons for retaining

---

[1] The name occurs in a dozen different forms in the ancient records. I adopt the form which is generally used by modern French writers. D'Argentré and other historians of Brittany say that it was not unknown about Nantes in those days. We must remember that it was the period when nicknames, trade-names, etc., were passing into surnames. Another pun on the name, which greatly tickled the mediæval imagination, was 'Aboilar,' supposed to convey the idea that he was a dog who barks at heaven (*aboie le ciel*). It was perpetrated by Hugo Metellus, a rival master.

the historical framework of the anecdote. It is a fact that Abélard never mastered mathematics ; chancing to mention arithmetic in one of his works, he says, 'Of that art I confess myself wholly ignorant.' It was unfortunate for mathematics. Most probably the puerility of that liberal art, in its early mediæval form, repelled him. In the next place, there was a distinguished master living in France of the name of Tirric, or Theodoric, who is said to have had a leaning to mathematics. He taught in the episcopal school at Chartres, long famous for the lectures of his brother Bernard. Finally, a Master Tirric (presumably the same) turns up at Abélard's trial in 1121, and boldly and caustically scourges papal legate and bishops alike. However, if we attribute so much authority to the story, it clearly refers to a later date. The picture of Abélard, already a teacher, sated with knowledge, coming ' in private ' to repair an omission in the course of his studies, must be relegated to one of the intervals in his teaching at Paris, not, as Mr. Poole thinks, to the period between leaving Roscelin and arriving at Paris.

Abélard himself merely says that he 'went wherever dialectics flourished.' For five or six

years he wandered from school to school, drawn
onward continually by the fame of schools and of
masters. Schools were plentiful, and the age was
already rich in great teachers. Charlemagne had
inaugurated the scholastic age two hundred years
before with the founding of the Palace School,
and had directed that every monastery and every
episcopal town should give instruction. With
periods of languor the Benedictines had sustained
the scholastic tradition through the soulless age
that followed, and the second half of the eleventh
century saw a brisk development. There was
the great abbey of Bec, in Normandy, where
St. Anselm still detained crowds of pupils after
the departure of Lanfranc. But at Bec the
students were not part of a 'great undisciplined
horde,' as Rashdall calls the students of the early
Middle Ages. With its careful regulations, its
bare-back castigations, its expurgated classics, and
its ever watchful monks, it contrived at once to
cultivate the mind (in moderation) and to guard
the sanctity of faith and morals. Cluny, in the
south, had a similar school at its gates, and the
same control of the scholars it lodged and fed.
St. Denis, near Paris, had another famous
Benedictine school. The forty monasteries that

William of Dijon had recently reformed had opened free schools for the wandering pupils, and even fed the poorer youths.

Then there were men of European fame teaching in the cathedral cloisters of the larger towns. At Chartres, good Bishop Ivo—the only lawyer who ever lived and died in the odour of sanctity—had spent much energy in the improvement of his school. Little John, or John of Salisbury, has left us a proud record of its life at a slightly later date, when Tirric and his brother Bernard presided over it. At Tournai, Master Eudes of Orleans, the peripatetic of the time, walked the cloisters all day with his questioning scholars, and gathered them before the cathedral door of an evening to explain the profound mysteries of the solid spheres that whirled overhead, and of the tiny, immortal fires that were set in them. Other famous episcopal schools were those of Tours, Rheims, Angers, and Laon. But every bishop had his master or masters for the teaching of grammar, rhetoric, and dialectics (the *trivium*), and in the larger towns were 'lectors' of the other four liberal arts (the *quadrivium*), music, geometry, arithmetic, and astronomy. Theology was taught under the watchful eye of the bishop and his chapter, and in time chairs of Hebrew, and, with the progress of the Saracenic invasion of the intellectual world, even of Arabic, were founded. At the abbey of St. Denis, monk Baldwin, sometime physician to the King of England, taught and practised the art of healing. At Chartres, also, medicine was taught somewhat later; and there are stories of teachers of law. And beside all these, there were the private masters, 'coaches,' etc., who opened schools wherever any number of scholars forgathered.

Thus the historical imagination can readily picture all that is contained in the brief phrase with which Abélard dismisses the five or six years of his studies. 'There was no regular curriculum in those days,' Mr. Rashdall says, in his study of the 'Universities of Europe'; but the seven liberal arts were taught, and were gradually arranging themselves in a series under the pressure of circumstances. Music Abélard certainly studied; before many years his songs were sung through the length and breadth of France. None of his contemporaries made a more eager and profitable study of what was called grammar—that is, not merely an exercise in the rules of Donatus and Priscian, but a close acquaintance with the

great Latin poets and historians. Rhetoric and
dialectics he revelled in—' I went wherever
dialectics flourished.' To so good purpose did
he advance in this work of loosening the tongue
and sharpening the wit, that throughout his life
the proudest orators and thinkers of Christendom
shrank in dismay from the thought of a verbal
encounter with him. ' I am a child beside him,'
pleaded Bernard of Clairvaux, at a time when
France, and even Rome, trembled at the sound
of his own voice. But we must defer for a few
pages the consideration of mediæval dialectics.

' Illi soli patuit quicquid scibile erat,'

said an ancient epitaph ; and, though the historian
handles epigrams with discretion, it must be
admitted that Abélard surpassed his contemporaries, not only in ability and in utterance, but
also in erudition. There is the one exception
of mathematics, but it seems probable that he
despised what passed under that name in the
twelfth century. ' Mathematics,' he says somewhere, in a sarcastic parenthesis, ' the exercise of
which is nefarious.' But in the thrust and parry
of dialectics he found a keen delight ; and so he
wandered from place to place, edging his logical

weapons on fellow-pupils and provincial masters, until one day, about the opening year of the twelfth century, he directed his steps towards far-famed Paris—beautiful, naughty, brilliant, seductive Paris, even in those distant days.

But the Paris of the first decade of the twelfth century was wholly different, not only from the Paris of to-day, but even from the Paris of Victor Hugo's famous picture.

CHAPTER II

A BRILLIANT VICTORY

IF you desire to see the Paris of those early days, imagine yourself beside the spot where the modern Pantheon stands. It is the summit of what Paris called ' the hill ' for many a century— the hill of St. Genevieve. Save for the large monastery of secular canons beside you, the abbey of St. Genevieve, there is yet little sign of the flood of grimy masonry that will creep up slowly from the river valley, as the ages advance, and foul the sweet country for miles beyond. Paris lies down in the valley below, a toy city. The larger island in the Seine bears almost the whole weight of the capital of France. It has, it is true, eaten a little way into the northern bank of the river, to which it is joined by the Great Bridge. That is the Lombard Quarter, and Lutetian commerce is increasing rapidly. Numbers of curious ships sail up the broad, silver bosom of the Seine, and make for the port of St. Landry. The commercial quarter is already spreading in the direction of Montmartre, with the public butchery and bakery at its outskirt ; but it is a mere fringe. The broad valleys and the gentle hills that are one day to support Paris are now clothed with vine-yards and orchards and cornfields, and crowned with groves of olive[1] and oak. On the nearer side, too, the city has already overflowed the narrow limits of the island. There are houses on the fine stone bridge, the Little Bridge, and there is a pretty confusion of houses, chapels, schools, and taverns gradually stealing up the slope of St. Genevieve. But, here also, most of the hill is covered with gardens and vineyards, from which a chapel or a relic of old Roman Lutetia peeps out here and there—the ruins of the famous old thermæ lie halfway down the hill below us—; and along the valley of the

' . . . florentibus ripis amnis '

(to quote a poet of the time), to east and west, are broad lakes of fresh green colour, broken only in their sweet monotony by an occasional island of

---

[1] This and other details I gather from fragments of the minor poets of the time.

masonry, an abbey with a cluster of cottages about it.

It is down straight below us, on the long, narrow island, that we see the heart of France, the centre of its political, intellectual, and ecclesiastical life. A broad, unpaved road, running from Great Bridge to Little Bridge, cuts it into two. Church occupies most of the eastern half, State most of the western ; their grateful subjects pack themselves as comfortably as they can in the narrow fringe that is left between the royal and ecclesiastical domains and the bed of the river. Each generation in turn has wondered why it was so scourged by 'the burning fire' (the plague), and resolved to be more generous to the Church. From the summit of St. Genevieve we see the front of the huge, grey, Roman cathedral, that goes back to the days of Childebert, and the residences of its prelates and canons bordering the cloister. Over against it, to the west, is the spacious royal garden, which is graciously thrown open to the people two or three times a week, with the palace of King Philip at the extremity of the island. That is Paris in the year of grace 1100 ; and all outside those narrow limits is a very dream of undulating scenery, with the vesture of the vine, the fir, the cypress, the oak, the olive, and the fig; and the colour of the rose, the almond, the lily, and the violet; and the broad, sweet Seine meandering through it; and the purest air that mortal could desire.

To our young philosopher Paris probably presented itself first in the character of 'the city of philosophers.' Each of the great abbeys had its school. That of the abbey of St. Genevieve will soon be familiar to us. The abbey of St. Germain of Auxerre, to the north, and the abbey of St. Germain of the Meadow, to the west, had schools at their gates for all comers. St. Martin in the Fields had its school, and the little priory of St. Victor, to the east, was soon to have one of the most famous of all schools of theology. The royal abbey of St. Denis, a few miles away, had a school in which Prince Louis was then being trained, together with the illustrious Abbot Suger. A number of private schools were scattered about the foot of St. Genevieve. The Jews had a school, and—mark the liberality of the time—there was, or had been until a very few years before, a school for women; it was conducted by the wife and daughters of famous Master Manegold, of Alsace, women who were well versed in Scripture, and 'most distinguished in philosophy,' says Muratori.

But Abélard went straight to the centre of Paris, to the cloistral enclosure under the shadow of old Notre Dame,[1] where was the first episcopal school in the kingdom, and one of the first masters in Christendom. William of Champeaux was a comparatively young master, who had forced his way into high places by sheer ability. He was held to be the first dialectician in France, and 'almost the first royal councillor.' In the great philosophic controversy of the period he was the leader of the orthodox school. The Bishop of Paris had brought him to the island-city, and vested him with the dignity of archdeacon of the cathedral and *scholasticus* (chancellor or rector) and master of the episcopal school. So high was the repute of his ability and his doctrine that, so Fleury says, he was called 'the pillar of doctors.' From an obscure local centre of instruction he had lifted the Parisian school into a commanding position, and had attracted scholars from many lands. And he was then in the prime of life. Within a few months Abélard made his

---

[1] The Notre Dame of to-day, like the earlier Louvre, dates from the end of the twelfth century.

authority totter, and set his reputation on the
wane. In six or seven years he drove him, in
shame and humiliation, from his chair, after a
contest that filled Christendom with its echoes.

Let us repeat that William of Champeaux was
then in the prime of life, or only ten years older
than Abélard. There are those who talk of the
'venerable teacher' and the audacious, irreverent
stripling. This picture of the conflict is his-
torically ridiculous. Rousselot and Michaud, two
of the most careful students of Champeaux's life,
give the date of his birth as 1068 and 1070,
respectively. He had fought his way with early
success into the first chair in Christendom; he
cannot have been much older than Abélard when
he secured it. Abélard had an immeasurably
greater ability; he was frankly conscious of the
fact; and he seems promptly to have formed the
perfectly legitimate design of ousting William—
whose philosophy certainly seemed absurd to him
—and mounting the great chair of Notre Dame.

Such a thought would naturally take shape
during the course of the following twelve months.
The only indication that Abélard gives us is to
the effect that William was well disposed towards
him at first, though there is no foundation in

recorded fact for the assertion that William invited the youth to his house, but they were gradually involved in a warm dialectical encounter. Abélard was not only a handsome and talented youth (which facts he candidly tells us himself), but he was a practised dialectician. The lectures of those untiring days lasted for hours, and might be interrupted at any moment by a question from a scholar. Moreover, William was principally occupied with dialectics, and it would be quite impossible—if it were desired—to instruct youths in the art of disputing, without letting them exercise their powers on the hosts of problems which served the purpose of illustration. Hence the young Breton must have quickly brought his keen rapier into play. The consciousness of power and the adolescent vanity of exhibiting it, both generously developed in Abélard, would prepare the way for ambition. Question and answer soon led on to a personal contest.

But there was a stronger source of provocation, and here it will be necessary to cast a hurried glance at the great controversy of the hour. Cousin has said that the scholastic philosophy was born of a phrase that Boetius translated out of Porphyry. It is a good epigram ; but it has the disadvantage of most epigrams—it is false. The controversy about *genera* and *species* is by no means of vital importance to the scholastic philosophy, as Abélard himself has said. However, there is much truth in the assertion that this celebrated controversy, as a specific question, may be traced entirely to Porphyry.

Boetius was the chief author read in the early mediæval schools. Amongst other works they had his Latin translation of Porphyry's *Introduction* to Aristotle, and in one corner of this volume some roving scholastic had been arrested by the allusion to the old Greek controversy about *genera* and *species*. To put it shortly : we have mental pictures of individual men, and we have also the idea of man in general, an idea which may be applied to each and all of the individual men we know. The grave problem that agitated the centuries was, whether not only the individual human beings who live and move about us, but also this 'general man' or species, had an existence outside the mind. The modern photographer has succeeded in taking composite photographs. A number of human likenesses are super-imposed on the same plate, so that at length individual features are blended, and there emerges only the vague portrait of 'a man.' The question that vexed the mediæval soul was, whether this human type, as distinct from the individual mortals we see in the flesh, had a real existence.

In whatever terms the problem be stated, it is sure to appear almost childish to the non-philosophical reader ; as, indeed, it appeared to certain scholars even of that time. John of Salisbury, with his British common sense and impatience of dialectical subtlety, petulantly spoke of it as 'the ancient question, in the solution of which the world has grown grey, and more time has been consumed than the Cæsars gave to the conquest and dominion of the globe, more money wasted than Crœsus counted in all his wealth.' But listen to another Briton, and one with the fulness of modern life outspread before him. Archbishop Roger Vaughan, defending the attitude of the enthusiasts in his *Thomas of Aquin*, says : 'Kill ideas, blast theories, explode the archetypes of things, and the age of brute force is not far distant.' And Rousselot declares, in his *Philosophie du Moyen Age*, that the problem of universals is 'the most exalted and the most difficult question in the whole of philosophy.' Poor philosophy !

will be the average layman's comment. However, though neither ancient Greeks nor mediæval formalists were guilty of the confusion of *ideas* and *ideals* which Dom Vaughan betrays, the schoolmen had contrived to connect the question in a curious fashion with the mystery of the Trinity.

When, therefore, Jean Roscelin began to probe the question with his dialectical weapons, the ears of the orthodox were opened wide. The only position which was thought compatible with the faith was realism—the notion that the species or the genus was a reality, distinct from the individuals that belonged to it, and outside the mind that conceived it. By and by it was whispered in the schools, and wandering scholars bore the rumour to distant monasteries and bishoprics, that Roscelin denied the real existence of these universals. Indeed, in his scorn of the orthodox position, he contemptuously declared them to be ' mere words '; neither in the world of reality, nor in the mind itself, was there anything corresponding to them ; they were nothing but an artifice of human speech. Europe was ablaze at once. St. Anselm assailed the heretic from the theological side ; William of Champeaux stoutly led the opposition, and the defence of realism, from the side of philosophy. Such was the question of the hour, such the condition of the world of thought, when Pierre Abélard reached the cloistral school at Paris.

If you stated the problem clearly to a hundred men and women who were unacquainted with philosophic speculations, ninety-nine of them would probably answer that these universals were neither mere words nor external realities, but general or generalised ideas—composite photographs, to use the interesting comparison of Mr. Galton, in the camera of the mind. That was the profound discovery with which Abélard shattered the authority of his master, revolutionised the thought of his age, and sent his fame to the ends of the earth. He had introduced a new instrument into the dialectical world, common sense, like the little girl in the fairy tale, who was brought to see the prince in his imaginary clothes.[1] This, at least, Abélard achieved, and it was a brilliant triumph for the unknown youth : he swept for ever out of the world of thought, in spite of almost all the scholars of Christendom,

---

[1] Lest there be a suspicion of caricature, or of ignorance (though I too have sat in the chair of scholastic philosophy, and held grave discourse on *genera* and *species*), let me remind the reader of the theological import which was read into the problem.

that way of thinking and of speaking which is
known as realism.   I am familiar with the opinion
of scholastic thinkers in this question, from the
thirteenth century to the present day.   It differs
verbally, but not substantially, from the con-
ceptualism of Abélard.   The stripling of twenty
or twenty-one had enunciated the opinion which
the world of thought was to adopt.

We still have some of the arguments with
which Abélard assailed his chief—but enough of
philosophy, let us proceed with the story.   Once
more the swift and animated years are condensed
into a brief phrase by the gloomy autobiographist ;
though there is a momentary flash of the old spirit
when he says of the earlier stage that he ' seemed
at times to have the victory in the dispute,' and
when he describes the final issue in the words of
Ovid,

    ' . . . non sum superatus ab illo.'

He soon found the weak points in William's
armour, and proceeded to attack him with the
uncalculating passion of youth.   It was not long
before the friendly master was converted into a
bitter, life-long enemy ; and that, he wearily
writes, ' was the beginning of my calamities.'
Possibly : but it is not unlikely that he had had

a similar experience at Locmenach. However that may be, it was a fatal victory. Ten years afterwards we find William in closest intimacy and daily intercourse with Bernard of Clairvaux.

Most of the scholars at Notre Dame were incensed at the success of Abélard. In those earlier days the gathering was predominantly clerical; the more so, on account of William's championship of orthodoxy. But as the controversy proceeded, and rumour bore its echo to the distant schools, the number and the diversity of the scholars increased. Many of the youths took the side of the handsome, brilliant young noble, and encouraged him to resist. He decided to open a school.

There was little organisation in the schools at that period — the university not taking shape until fully sixty years afterwards (Compayré)— and Abélard would hardly need a 'license' for the purpose, outside the immediate precincts of the cloister. But William was angry and powerful. It were more discreet, at least, not to create a direct and flagrant opposition to him. The little group of scholars moved to Melun, and raised a chair for their new master in that royal town. It was thirty miles away, down the valley of the Seine; but a thirty mile walk was a trifle in the days when railways were unknown, and William soon noticed a leakage in his class. Moreover, Melun was an important town, the king spending several months there every year. William made strenuous efforts to have the new academy suppressed, but he seems to have quarrelled with some of the courtiers, and these took up the cause of the new master of noble rank.

When Abélard saw the powerlessness of the chancellor of Notre Dame, he decided to come a little nearer. There was another fortified and royal town, Corbeil by name, about half-way to Paris, and thither he transferred his chair and his followers. The move was made, he tells us, for the convenience of his students. His reputation was already higher than William's, and the duel of the masters had led to a noisy conflict between their respective followers. Corbeil being a comfortable day's walk from Paris, there was a constant stream of rival pupils flowing between the two. In the schools and the taverns, on the roads and the bridges, nothing was heard but the increasing jargon of the junior realists and conceptualists. Besides the great problem, dialectics had countless lesser ones that would furnish argumentative material for an eternity. ' Whether the pig that is being driven to market is held by the man or the rope'; 'whether a shield that is white on one side and black on the other may be called either black or white,' and problems of that kind, are not to be compared in point of depth and fecundity with such mere matters of fact as the origin of species. But the long and severe strain had gravely impaired Abélard's health; he was compelled to close his school, and return to Brittany. William was not the only one who rejoiced. The Church was beginning to view with some alarm the spread of the new doctrine and the new spirit. Cynical rivals were complaining that ' the magician ' had brought ' a plague of frogs' on the land.

Abélard tells us that he remained ' for several years almost cut off from France.' Rémusat thinks it was probably during this period that he studied under Roscelin, but there is now little room for doubt that his intercourse with the famous nominalist falls in the earlier years. Much more probable is it that we should assign his relations to Tirric of Chartres to the later date. The substance of the anecdote that was

found on the margin of the Ratisbon manuscript
seems to accord admirably with Abélard's circumstances in the period we have now reached.
The question, however, will interest few, beyond
the narrow circle of historical specialists. He
himself is silent about the few years of rest in
the Breton castle, merely stating that he returned
to Paris when he had recovered his health. We
have to remember that the autobiography he has
left us was entitled by him the 'Story of my
Calamities.' It is not the full presentment of the
swiftly moving drama of the life of Abélard.
He speaks of joy only when it is the prelude to
sorrow, or when some faint spark of the old
ardour leaps into life once more.

When Abélard at length returned to the arena,
he found a significant change. William had
deserted the cloistral school. In a solitary spot
down the river, beyond the foot of the eastern
slope of St. Genevieve, was a small priory that
had belonged to the monks of St. Victor of
Marseilles. Thither, says Franklin, William had
retired ' to hide his despair and the shame of his
defeat.' The controversy had by no means been
decided against him yet. Indeed, William's
biographers loyally contend that he was sincerely

touched by the religious spirit of the age, and adopted the monastic life from the purest of motives. Abélard, on the other hand, declares that the inspiration came from a hope of exchanging the chair of Notre Dame for that of an episcopal see. Abélard is scarcely an ideal witness, though the passage was written nearly thirty years afterwards, yet his interpretation is probably correct; at least, if we take it as a partial explanation. William was shrewd enough to see that his supremacy in the scholastic world was doomed, and that the best alternative was a bishopric. He was still young (about thirty-eight, apparently) and ambitious; in his character of archdeacon, he was already only one step removed from the episcopate; and he had influence and qualifications above the average. It is scarcely correct to say, as Gervaise does, that at that time 'the monastery was the recognised path to the episcopacy,' on account of the wide degradation of the secular clergy. Their degradation was assuredly deep and wide-spread, but so were simony and electoral corruption. We generally find, in the old chronicles, one or other of the deceased bishop's archdeacons ascending the vacant throne. However, William of Champeaux was a religious man; for the pious the surest path to the episcopate passed through the monastery.

Whatever be the correct analysis of the motive —and it was probably a complex feeling, including all the impulses suggested, which William himself scarcely cared to examine too narrowly—the fact is that in the year 1108 he donned the black cassock of the canon regular, and settled with a few companions in the priory of St. Victor. The life of the canons regular was a compromise between that of the sterner monks and the un-ascetic life of the secular canons and secular clergy. They followed, on the whole, the well-known rule of St. Augustine. They arose at midnight to chant their matins, but, unlike the Cistercians, they returned to bed as soon as the 'office' was over. They ate meat three times a week, and were not restricted in the taking of fish and eggs. They had linen underclothing, and much friendly intercourse with each other, and they were less rigidly separated from the world. Altogether, not too rough a path to higher dignities—or to heaven—and (a not un-important point) one that did not lead far from Paris.

Such was the foundation of one of the most famous schools of mystic theology. The abbey that William instituted, before he was removed to the coveted dignity in 1113, has attained an immortality in the world of thought through such inmates as Richard and Hugh of St. Victor.

Abélard's first impulse on hearing the news was to repair at once to the cloistral school. He found the chair occupied. William had not, in fact, resigned his title of scholastic, and he had placed a substitute in the chair. It was a poor ruse, for there was now no master in Christendom who could long endure the swift, keen shafts of the ambitious Breton. Abélard would quickly make the chair of Notre Dame uncomfortable for the most pachydermatous substitute; and he seems to have commenced the edifying task at once, when he heard that the unfortunate William had set up a chair of rhetoric at St. Victor. Like a hawk, Master Peter descended on the ill-fated canon. The Bishop of Mans had, it appears, stimulated William into a renewal of activity, and he had chosen that apparently safe section of the trivium, the art of rhetoric.

With what must have been a mock humility, Abélard went down the river each day with the

crowd of monks and clerks to receive instruction
in rhetoric from the new Prior of St. Victor's.
Deutsch remarks, with Teutonic gravity, that
we do not read of a reconciliation between the
two.   Nor do we find that Abélard had been
'converted' to the spirit of Robert of Arbrissel
or Bernard of Clairvaux during his retirement
at Pallet.   Abélard, now nearly thirty years of
age, could have taught William the art of
rhetoric with more profit than he himself was
likely to derive from William's *prælectiones*.   His
obvious aim was to break William's connection
with Paris and with Notre Dame.   The high
and gentle spirit of these latter days, that studies
the feelings of an antagonist, and casts aside an
ambition that would lead over the fallen fame of
a fellow-man, did not commend itself to the
mediæval mind.

And so the contest ran on, until at length a
new rumour was borne over the roads and into
the schools of Europe.   The 'pillar of doctors'
was broken — had fallen beyond restoration.
Guillaume de Champeaux had changed his doctrine
on the question of universals.   Swiftly the story
ran over hill and dale—they were days when the
words of masters outstripped the deeds of kings

and the fall of dynasties : the champion of realism
had so far yielded to Abélard's pressure as to
modify his thesis materially.   For long years he
had held that the universal was *essentially* one and
the same in all its individuals ; now he admitted
that it was only *indifferently*, or *individually*,
identical.[1]   The death of King Philip was a matter
of minor interest to a world that brooded night
and day over the question of genera and species.

Abélard felt that he need strive no longer in
the hall of the poor canon regular, and he turned
his attention to the actual occupant of the chair
of Notre Dame.   We need not delay in determining the name of the luckless master, whether
it was Robert of Melun, as some think, or Adam
of the Little Bridge, or Peter the Eater—poor
man ! a sad name to come down the ages with ;
it was merely an allusion to his voracious reading.
He had the saving grace of common-sense,
whatever other gifts he was burdened with.   As
soon as he saw the collapse of William's authority
and the dispersal of his pupils, he resolved to
decline a contest with the irresistible Breton.

[1] The reader would probably not be grateful for a long explanation of the meaning of the change.   It amounted to a considerable
approach of William's position towards that of Abélard.

He voluntarily yielded the chair to Abélard, and took his place on the hay-strewn floor amongst the new worshippers. Such a consummation, however, was not to the taste of the angered scholastic. A substitute had, it seems, the power to subdelegate his license, so that the installation of Abélard in the cathedral school was correct and canonical. But William was still scholastic of the place, and he had an obvious remedy. Robert, or Peter, or whoever it may have been, depended on him, and he at once set to work to recall the delegation. Abélard says that he trumped up a false and most obnoxious charge against the intermediary. He did, at all events, succeed in changing the appointment, and thus rendering Abélard's subdelegated license null. The new-comer was a man of different temper, so that Abélard only occupied the great chair 'for a few days.' He could not teach in or about the episcopal school without a 'respondent,' and he therefore once more transferred his chair to Melun.[1]

The Prior of St. Victor's had won a pyrrhic

[1] To transfer a chair was frequently a physical operation in those days. There is, in one of the old records, a story of a dissatisfied master and his pupils removing their chair to another town, higher up the river. They were not welcome, it seems, and their chair was pitched into the river to find its way home.

victory. Whether or no Abélard had learned a lesson from him, and began in his turn to practise the subtle art of diplomacy, we cannot say, but Paris was soon too warm for the prior. The lawless students respected his authority no longer, and clamoured for Abélard. The king was dead : long live the king! They discovered that William's conversion was peculiarly incomplete. For a man who had felt an inner call to leave the world, he still evinced a fairly keen interest in its concerns. William found their 'ceaseless raillery' intolerable. He fled, says Archbishop Roger Vaughan, 'to hide his shame in a distant monastery.' Abélard merely records that 'he transferred his community to a certain town at some distance from the city.' The path to Paris lay open once more.

CHAPTER III

PROGRESS OF THE ACADEMIC WAR

WHEN Abélard and his admirers returned from Melun to Paris, they found William's new successor sitting resolutely in the chair of Notre Dame.   From some manuscripts of the 'Story of my Calamities' it appears that he had won repute by his lectures on Priscian, the Latin grammarian. He had thus been able to augment the little band who remained faithful to William and to orthodoxy with a certain number of personal admirers. Clearly, the episcopal school must be taken by storm.   And so, says Abélard, his pen leaping forward more quickly at the recollection, twenty years afterwards, 'we pitched our camp on the hill of St. Genevieve.'

During the century that preceded the coalescence of the schools into a university, St. Genevieve was the natural home of rebellion.   Roscelin had taught there.   Joscelin the Red, another famous nominalist, was teaching there. The 'feminists' had raised their tabernacle there ; the Jews their synagogue. From its physical advantages the hill naturally presented itself to the mind of every master who had designs on the episcopal school or the episcopal philosophy. Its gentle, sunny flanks offered ideal situations for schools, and the students were breaking away more and more from the vicinity of the cloister and the subordination it expressed. A new town was rapidly forming at its foot, by the river, and on the northern slope ; a picturesque confusion of schools, chapels, brothels, taverns, and hospices. It was the cradle of the famed Latin Quarter—*very* Latin in those days, when the taverns swung out their Latin signs, 'taverna de grangia,' 'ad turbotum,' 'apud duos cygnos,' and so forth, and the songs that came from the latticed, vine-clothed arbours were half French, half Celtic-Latin.

Abélard did not open a private school on 'the hill.' He delivered his assault on 'the island' from the abbey of St. Genevieve at the summit, the site now occupied by the Pantheon. There is nothing in the least remarkable in the abbey opening its gates to one who was obviously bent on assailing the great ecclesiastical school, and who was already regarded as the parent of a new and freer generation of students. The secular canons had little deference for authority and little love of asceticism at that period. St. Norbert had fruitlessly tried to reform them, and had been forced to embody his ideal in a new order. Cardinal Jacques de Vitry, the classical censor of the twelfth century, makes bitter comment on their hawks and horses, their jesters and singing-girls, and their warmer than spiritual affection for their sisters in religion, the ' canonesses.' It was natural enough that an abbey of secular canons should welcome the witty and brilliant young noble— and the wealth that accompanied him.

We have little information about the abbey at that precise date, but history has much to say of its affairs some thirty or forty years afterwards, and thus affords a retrospective light. In the year 1146 Innocent the Second paid a visit to Paris. The relics of St. Genevieve were one of the treasures of the city, and thither his holiness went with his retinue, and King Louis and his followers. In the crush that was caused in the abbey church, the servants of the canons quarrelled with those of the court, and one of them was unlucky enough to bring his staff down with some force

on the royal pate. That was a death-blow to the
gay life of the abbey. Paris, through the abbot
of St. Denis, who was also the first royal councillor, quickly obtained royal and papal assent to
the eviction of the canons, and they were soon
summarily turned out on the high road. They
did not yield without a struggle, it is true. Many
a night afterwards, when the canons regular who
replaced them were in the midst of their solemn
midnight chant, the evicted broke in the doors of
the church, and made such turmoil inside, that the
chanters could not hear each other across the
choir. And when they did eventually depart for
less rigorous surroundings, they thoughtfully took
with them a good deal of the gold from Genevieve's
tomb and other ecclesiastical treasures, which were
not reclaimed until after many adventures.

To this abbey of St. Genevieve, then, the mili-
tant master led his followers, and he began at
once to withdraw the students from Notre Dame,
as he candidly tells us. If Bishop Galo and his
chapter found their cloistral school deserted, they
might be induced to consider Abélard's gifts and
influence. So the war went on merrily between
the two camps. The masters fulminated against
each other ; the students ran from school to school,

and argued it out on the bridge and in the taverns, and brought questions to their logical conclusion in the Pré-aux-clercs.[1] There was certainly, as we saw previously, ample room for litigation in the problems of mediæval dialectics. John of Salisbury studied dialectics under Abélard at St. Genevieve (though not in the abbey) at a later date, and he tells us that when he returned to Paris twelve years afterwards he found his dialectical friends just where he had left them. 'They had not added the smallest proposition,' he says contemptuously. Little John preferred 'philology,' as they called classical studies in his day.

We get a curious insight into the school-life of the period in the *Life of Saint Goswin*. Goswin of Douai—whom we shall meet again once or twice—was studying in the school of Master Joscelin the Red, down the hill. He was a youthful saint of the regulation pattern : had borne the aureole from his cradle. About this time he is described as brimming over with precocious zeal for righteousness, and astounded at the impunity with which Abélard poured out his novelties.

---

[1] Until a comparatively recent date 'aller sur le Pré' meant, in the language of the Latin Quarter, to settle an affair of honour.

Why did not some one silence 'this dog who barked at the truth'?   Already, the authors of the saint's life—two monks of the twelfth century— say, 'Abélard's hand was against every man, and every man's hand against him,' yet no one seemed inclined 'to thrash him with the stick of truth.' The young saint could not understand it.   He went to Master Joscelin at length, and declared that he was going to do the work of the Lord himself.   Joscelin is reported to have endeavoured to dissuade him with a feeling description of Abélard's rhetorical power; we do not know, however, that Joscelin was void of all sense of humour.   In any case the saintly youngster of 'modest stature' with the 'blue-grey eyes and light air' had a good measure of courage.   It will be interesting, perhaps, to read the issue in the serio-comic language of the times.

'With a few companions he ascended the hill of St. Genevieve, prepared, like David, to wage single conflict with the Goliath who sat there thundering forth strange novelties of opinion to his followers and ridiculing the sound doctrine of the wise.

'When he arrived at the battlefield—that is, when he entered the school—he found the master giving his lecture and instilling his novelties into his hearers. But as soon as he began to speak, the master cast an angry look at him; knowing himself to be a warrior from his youth, and noticing that the scholar was beginning to feel nervous, he despised him in his heart. The youth was, indeed, fair and handsome of appearance, but slender of body and short of stature. And when the proud one was urged to reply, he said: "Hold thy peace, and disturb not the course of my lecture."'

The story runs, however, that Abélard's students represented to him that the youth was of greater importance than he seemed to be, and persuaded him to take up the glove. 'Very well,' said Abélard, and it is not improbable, 'let him say what he has to say.' It was, of course, unfortunate for Goliath, as the young champion of orthodoxy, aided by the Holy Spirit, completely crushed him in the midst of his own pupils.

'The strong man thus bound by him who had entered his house, the victor, who had secured the Protean-changing monster with the unfailing cord of truth, descended the hill. When they had come to the spot where their companions awaited them in the distant schools [*i.e.* when they had got to a safe distance from Abélard's pupils], they burst forth in pæans of joy and triumph : humbled was the tower of pride, downcast was the wall of contumacy, fallen was he that had scoffed at Israel, broken was the anvil of the smiter,' etc. etc.

The course of events does not seem to have been much influenced by this breaking of the 'anvil.' Joscelin was soon compelled to seek fresh pastures ; he also found ultimate consolation in a bishopric, and a share in the condemnation of Abélard. The commentator of Priscian must then have received the full force of Abélard's keen dialectical skill and mordant satire. His students began to fall away to the rival camp in large numbers. William was informed in his distant solitude, and he returned ('impudenter,' says Abélard) in haste to St. Victor's. He opened his old school in the priory, and for a time Paris rang more loudly than ever with the dialectical battle. But William's intervention proved fatal to his cause. The substitute had kept a handful of students about him, Abélard says, but even they disappeared when William returned. The poor Priscianist could think of nothing better than to develop 'a call to the monastic life,' and he obeyed it with admirable alacrity.   However, just as Abélard was about to enter on the last stage of the conflict, he was recalled to Pallet by his mother.

The eleventh century had witnessed a strong revival of the monastic spirit.   When men came at length to feel the breath of an ideal in their souls, the sight of the fearful disorder of the age stimulated them to the sternest sacrifices.   They believed that he who said, 'If thou wilt be perfect, go and sell that thou hast, and give to the poor,' was God, that he meant what he said, and that he spoke the message to all the ages.   So there uprose a number of fervent preachers, whose voices thrilled with a strange passion, and they burned the Christ-message into the souls of men and women.   In Brittany and Normandy Robert of Arbrissel and two or three others had been at work years before St. Bernard began his apostolate.   They had broken up thousands of homes —usually those which were helping most to sweeten the life of the world—and sent husband and wife to spend their days apart in monasteries and nunneries.   The modern world speaks of the harshness of it; in their thoughts it was only a salutary separation for a time, making wholly certain their speedy reunion in a not too ethereal heaven. In the great abbey of Fontevraud, founded by Robert of Arbrissel in the year 1100, there were nearly four thousand nuns, a large proportion of whom were married women. Even in their own day the monastic orators were strongly opposed on account of their appalling dissolution of domestic ties. Roscelin attacked Robert of Arbrissel very warmly on the ground that he received wives into his monasteries against the will of their husbands, and in defiance of the command of the Bishop of Angers to release them: he boldly repeats the charge in a letter to the Bishop of Paris in 1121. Not only sober thinkers and honest husbands would resent the zeal of the Apostle of Brittany; the courtly, and the ecclesiastical and monastic, gallants of the time would be equally angry with him. We have another curious objection in some of the writers of the period. Answering the question why men were called to the monastic life so many centuries before women, they crudely affirm that the greater frailty of the women had made them less competent to meet the moral dangers of the cenobitic life. Thus from one cause or other a number of calumnies, still found in the chronicles, were in circulation about Robert of Arbrissel.[1]   It would be interesting to know what half-truths there were at the root of these charges ; there may have been such, in those days, quite consistently with perfect religious sincerity.   In the martyrologies of some of the monastic orders, there are women mentioned with high praise who disguised themselves as men, and lived for years in monasteries.   It is noteworthy that mediæval folk worked none of those miracles at the tomb of Robert of Arbrissel that they wrought at the tombs of St. Bernard and St. Norbert.   He is not a canonised saint.

However, in spite of both responsible and irresponsible opposition, Robert of Arbrissel, Vitalis the Norman, and other nervous orators, had caused an extensive movement from the hearth to the cloister throughout Brittany and Normandy, such as St. Bernard inaugurated in France later on.

---

[1] As a mere illustration of the times—no one would think of taking it seriously—we may quote the passage referring to him in Dubois's *Historia ecclesiae Parisiensis* (also found in Lobineau).   A monk and bishop, Gaufridus Vindoniencensis, writes to remonstrate with Robert for 'inventing a new kind of martyrdom' . . . 'inter feminas et cum ipsis noctu frequenter cubare.   Hinc tibi videris, ut asseris, Domini Salvatoris digne bajulare crucem, cum extinguere conaris male accensum carnis ardorem.'   Later he complains of Robert's partiality, treating some nuns with unusual sweetness and others with excessive acrimony; and amongst the punishments inflicted on the latter he mentions the penance of ' stripping.'

Home after home—*château* or *chaumière*—was left
to the children, and they who had sworn com-
panionship in life and death cheerfully parted in
the pathetic trust of a reunion.   Abélard's father
was touched by the sacred fire, and entered a
monastery.   His wife had to follow his example.
Whatever truth there was in the words of Roscelin,
the Church certainly commanded that the arrangement should be mutual, unless the lady were of
an age or a piety beyond suspicion, as St. Francis
puts it in his ' Rule.'   Lucia had agreed to take
the veil after her husband's departure.   This was
the news that withheld the hand of ' the smiter '
on the point of dealing a decisive blow, and he
hastened down to Brittany to bid farewell to his
' most dear mother.'   Not only in this expression,
but in the fact of his making the journey at all in
the circumstances, we have evidence of a profound
affection.   Since he had long ago abdicated his
rights of primogeniture, there cannot have been
an element of business in the visit to Pallet.

He was not long absent from Paris.   The
news reached him in Brittany that the prior had
at length discovered a dignified retreat from the
field.   Soon after Abélard's departure the bishopric
of Châlons-sur-Marne became vacant, and William

was nominated for the see.   He bade a fond farewell to Paris and to dialectics.   From that date
his ability was devoted to the safe extravagances
of mystic theology, under the safe tutorship of
St. Bernard.[1]   He had left his pupil Gilduin to
replace him at St. Victor, and the school quickly
assumed a purely theological character ; but the
luckless chair of Notre Dame he entrusted to the
care of Providence.

Abélard now formed a resolution which has
given rise to much speculation.   Instead of
stepping at once into the chair of the cloistral
school, which he admits was offered to him, he
goes off to some distance from Paris for the
purpose of studying theology.   It is the general
opinion of students of his life that his main object
in doing so was to make more secure his progress
towards the higher ecclesiastical dignities.   That
he had such ambition, and was not content with
the mere chair and chancellorship of the cloistral
school, is quite clear.   In his clouded and em-

---

[1] It will interest many, however, to learn (from the pages of
Du Boulai's *Historia Universitatis Parisiensis*) that he is charged by
the querulous Gaufridus Vindoniencensis with teaching that only the
gravest sins were matter for obligatory confession.   These particularly
grave transgressions are heresy, schism, paganism, and Judaism—all
non-ethical matters !

bittered age he is said, on the high authority of
Peter of Cluny, to have discovered even that final
virtue of humility.　There are those who prefer
him in the days of his frank, buoyant pride and
ambition.　If he had been otherwise in the days
of the integrity of his nature, he would have been
an intolerable prig.　He was the ablest thinker
and speaker in France.　He was observant enough
to perceive it, and so little artificial as to acknow-
ledge it, and act in accordance.　Yet there was
probably more than the counsel of ambition in his
resolution.　From the episode of Goswin's visit
to St. Genevieve it is clear that whispers of faith,
theology, and heresy were already breaking upon
the freedom of his dialectical speculations.　He
must have recalled the fate of Scotus Erigena,
of Bérenger, of Roscelin, and other philosophic
thinkers.　Philosophic thought was subtly linked
with ecclesiastical dogma.　He who contemplated
a life of speculation and teaching could not afford
to be ignorant of the ecclesiastical claims on and
limitations of his sphere.　Such thoughts can
scarcely have been unknown to him during the
preceding year or two, and it seems just and
reasonable to trace the issue of them in his resolution.　He himself merely says : ' I returned

chiefly for the purpose of studying divinity.'
Hausrath quotes a passage from his *Introductio
ad theologiam* with the intention of making Abélard
ascribe his resolution to the suggestion of his
admirers. On careful examination the passage
seems to refer to his purpose of writing on
theology, not to his initial purpose of studying it.

Abélard would naturally look about for the
first theological teacher in France. There were,
in point of fact, few theological chairs at that
time, but there was at least one French theologian
who had a high reputation throughout Christendom. Pupil of St. Anselm of Canterbury at Bec,
canon and dean of the town where he taught,
Anselm of Laon counted so many brilliant scholars
amongst his followers that he has been entitled
the 'doctor of doctors.' William of Champeaux,
William of Canterbury, and a large number of
distinguished masters, sat at his feet. His *scholia*
to the Vulgate were in use in the schools for
centuries. He and his brother Raoul had made
Laon a most important focus of theological activity
for more countries than France. England was
well represented there. John of Salisbury frequently has occasion to illustrate the fame and
magnitude of the cathedral school.

Anselm had been teaching for forty years when Abélard, *aetat.* thirty-four, appeared amidst the crowd of his hearers. We can well conceive the fluttering of wings that must have occurred, but Laon was not Paris, and Anselm was not the man to enter upon an argumentative conflict with the shrewd-tongued adventurer. Two incidents of contemporary life at Laon, in which Anselm figured, will be the best means of illustrating the character of the theologian. Abbot Guibertus, of that period, has left us a delightful work ' *De vita sua*,' from which we learn much about Laon and Anselm. The treasure of the cathedral was entrusted, it seems, to seven guardians—four clerics and three laymen. One of these guardians, a Canon Anselm, was a wolf in sheep's clothing. He purloined a good deal of the treasure ; and when the goldsmith, his accomplice, was detected, and turned king's evidence, Anselm denied the story, challenged the goldsmith to the usual duel, and won.[1] The canon was encouraged, and shortly set up as an expert burglar. One dark,

---

[1] When Anselm's guilt was ultimately proved, people were somewhat troubled as to the ill-success of their Providential detective service, until they heard that the goldsmith, in accusing the canon, had broken faith with him.

stormy night he went with his 'ladders and machines' to a tower in which much treasure was kept, and 'cracked' it. There was dreadful ado in the city next day; most horrible of all, the burglar had stolen a golden dove which contained some of the hair and some of the milk of the Virgin Mary. In the uncertainty the sapient Master Anselm (no relation, apparently, of Canon Anselm Beessus, the burglar and cathedral treasurer) was invited to speak. His advice largely reveals the man. Those were the days, it must be remembered, when the defects of the detective service were compensated by a willingness and activity of the higher powers which are denied to this sceptical age. When their slender police resources were exhausted, the accused was handed over to a priest, to be prepared, by prayer and a sober diet of bread, herbs, salt, and water, for the public ordeal. On the fourth day priests and people repaired to the church, and when the mass was over, and the vested priests had prostrated themselves in the sanctuary, the accused purged himself of the charge or proved his guilt by carrying or walking on a nine foot bar of heated iron, plunging his arms 'for an ell and a half' into boiling water, or being bodily immersed in a huge tank, cold, and carefully blessed and consecrated.

These are familiar facts. The difficulty at Laon was that there was no accused to operate on. The Solomon Laudunensis was therefore called into judgment, and his proposal certainly smacks of the thoroughness of the systematic theologian. A baby was to be taken from each parish of the town, and tried by the ordeal of immersion. When the guilty parish had been thus discovered, each family in it was to purge itself by sending an infant representative to the tank. When the guilt had been thus fastened on a certain house, all its inmates were to be put to the ordeal.[1]

We see Anselm in a very different light in an incident that occurred a year or two before Abélard's arrival. Through the influence of the King of England and the perennial power of gold a wholly unworthy bishop had been thrust upon

[1] Luckily the citizen-parents were wiser than their Solomon for once. They proposed that the process should commence with the seven treasurers. In spite of preliminary experiments in private the canon was convicted. But the reader must go to the pious Geoffroy's narrative (*Migne*, vol. 156, col. 1011) to read how the burglar was tortured, how he obtained release for a time by trickery, and how, being unable to sleep at night for a miraculous dove, he finally confessed and restored.

the people of Laon.   Illiterate, worldly, and much
addicted to military society, he was extremely
distasteful to Anselm and the theologians. The
crisis came when the English king, Henry i.,
tried to levy a tax on the people of Laon. The
bishop supported his patron ; Anselm and others
sternly opposed the tax in the name of the people.
Feeling ran so high that the bishop was at length
brutally murdered by some of the townsfolk, and
the cathedral was burned to the ground.   Anselm
immediately, and almost alone, went forth to de-
nounce the frenzied mob, and had the unfortunate
prelate—left for the dogs to devour before his
house—quietly buried.

Such was the man whom Abélard chose as his
next, and last, 'teacher.'   In the circumstances
revealed in the above anecdotes it would have
been decidedly dangerous to attack Anselm in
the manner that had succeeded so well at Notre
Dame.   There is, however, no just reason for
thinking that Abélard had formed an intention
of that kind.   No doubt, it is impossible to
conceive Abélard in the attitude of one who
seriously expected instruction from a master.
Yet it would be unjust to assume that he approached the class-room of the venerable, authori-

tative theologian in the same spirit in which he
had approached William of Champeaux's lectures
on rhetoric. We do not find it recorded that
he made any attempt to assail directly the high
position of the old man. It was sufficient for
the purpose we may ascribe to him that he should
be able to state in later years that he had fre-
quented the lectures of Anselm of Laon.

With whatever frame of mind the critic came
to Laon, he was not long in discovering the
defects of Anselm's teaching. Anselm had one
gift, a good memory, and its fruit, patristic
erudition. The fame that was borne over seas
and mountains was founded mainly on the marvellous wealth of patristic opinion which he applied
to every text of Scripture. There was no in-
dividuality, no life, in his work. To Abélard
the mnemonic feat was a mechanical matter ; and
indeed, he probably cared little at that time how
St. Ambrose or St. Cyril may have interpreted
this or that text. Little as he would be disposed
to trust the fame of masters after his experience,
he tells us that he was disappointed. He found
the ' fig-tree to be without fruit,' fair and promising as it had seemed. The lamp, that was
said to illumine theological Christendom, ' merely

filled the house with smoke, not light.' He found, in the words of his favourite Lucan,

> 'magni nominis umbra,
> Qualis frugifero quercus sublimis in agro' :

and he determined 'not to remain in this idleness under its shade very long.' With his usual heedlessness he frankly expressed his estimate of the master to his fellow pupils.

One day when they were joking together at the end of the lecture, and the students were twitting him with his neglect of the class, he quietly dropped a bomb to the effect that he thought masters of theology were superfluous. With the text and the ordinary glosses any man of fair intelligence could study theology for himself. He was contemptuously invited to give a practical illustration of his theory. Abélard took the sneer seriously, and promised to lecture on any book of Scripture they cared to choose. Continuing the joke, they chose the curious piece of Oriental work that has the title of Ezechiel. Once more Abélard took them seriously, asked for the text and gloss, and invited them to attend his first lecture, on the most abstruse of the prophets, on the following day. Most of them persisted in treating the matter as a joke, but a few appeared at the appointed spot (in Anselm's own territory) on the following day. They listened in deep surprise to a profound lecture on the prophet from the new and self-consecrated 'theologus.' The next day there was a larger audience ; the lecture was equally astonishing. In fine, Abélard was soon in full sail as a theological lector of the first rank, and a leakage was noticed in Anselm's lecture hall.

Abélard's theological success at Laon was brief, if brilliant. Two of the leading scholars, Alberic of Rheims and Lotulphe of Novare, urged Anselm to suppress the new movement at once. Seven years later we shall meet Alberic and Lotulphe playing an important part in the tragedy of Abélard's life ; later still Alberic is found in intimacy with St. Bernard. The episode of Laon must not be forgotten. Probably Anselm needed little urging, with the fate of William of Champeaux fresh in his ears. At all events he gave willing audience to the suggestion that a young master, without due theological training, might at any moment bring the disgrace of heresy on the famous school. He 'had the impudence to suppress me,' Abélard has the impudence to say.

The students are said to have been much angered by Anselm's interference, but there was no St. Genevieve at Laon — happily, perhaps, — and Abélard presently departed for Paris, leaving the field to the inglorious 'Pompey the Great.'

CHAPTER IV

THE IDOL OF PARIS

A NEW age began for Paris and for learning, when Peter Abélard accepted the chair of the episcopal school. It would be a difficult task to measure the influence he had in hastening the foundation of the university—as difficult as to estimate the enduring effect of his teaching on Catholic theology. There were other streams flowing into the life of the period, and they would have expanded and deepened it, independently of the activity of the one brilliant teacher. The work of a group of less gifted, though highly gifted, teachers had started a current of mental life which would have continued and broadened without the aid of Abélard. Life was entering upon a swifter course in all its reaches. Moreover, the slender rill of Greek thought, which formed the inspiration of the eleventh century, was beginning to increase. Through Alexandria, through Arabia, through Spain, the broad stream of the wisdom of the Greeks had been slowly travelling with the centuries. In the twelfth century it was crossing the Pyrenees, and stealing into the jealous schools of Europe. The homeless Jew was bringing the strong, swift, noble spirit of the 'infidel Moor' into a hideous world, that was blind with self-complacency. The higher works of Aristotle (the early Middle Ages had only his logic), the words of Plato, and so many others, were drifting into France. Christian scholars were even beginning to think of going to see with their own eyes this boasted civilisation of the infidel.

Yet it is clear that Abélard stands for a mighty force in the story of development. At the end of the eleventh century Paris was an island; at the end of the twelfth century it was a city of two hundred thousand souls, walled, paved, with several fine buildings and a fair organisation. At the end of the eleventh century the schools of Paris, scattered here and there, counted a few hundred pupils, chiefly French ; at the end of the twelfth century the University of Paris must have numbered not far short of ten thousand scholars. Let us see how much of this was effected by Abélard.

The pupil who had left Paris when both

E

William and Abélard disappeared in 1113 would find a marvellous change on returning to it about 1116 or 1117. He would find the lecture hall and the cloister and the quadrangle, under the shadow of the great cathedral, filled with as motley a crowd of youths and men as any scene in France could show. Little groups of French and Norman and Breton nobles chattered together in their bright silks and fur-tipped mantles, and with slender swords dangling from embroidered belts ; 'shaven in front like thieves, and growing luxuriant, curly tresses at the back like harlots,' growls Jacques de Vitry, who saw them, vying with each other in the length and crookedness of their turned-up shoes.[1] Anglo-Saxons looked on, in long fur-lined cloaks, tight breeches, and leathern hose swathed with bands of many coloured cloth. Stern-faced northerners, Poles, and Germans, in fur caps and coloured girdles and clumsy shoes, or with feet roughly tied up in the bark of trees, waited impatiently for the announcement of 'Li Mestre.' Pale-faced southerners had

[1] The Count of Anjou had just invented them to hide the enormity of his bunions. Flattering courtiers found them excellent. The English king's jester had exaggerated the turned-up points, and the nobles were driving the practice to death, as is the aristocratic wont.

braved the Alps and the Pyrenees under the fascination of 'the wizard.' Shaven and sandalled monks, black-habited clerics, black canons, secular and regular, black in face too, some of them, heresy-hunters from the neighbouring abbey of St. Victor, mingled with the crowd of young and old, grave and gay, beggars and nobles, sleek citizens and bronzed peasants.

Crevier and other writers say that Abélard had attracted five thousand students to Paris. Sceptics smile, and talk of Chinese genealogies. Mr. Rashdall, however, has made a careful study of the point, and he concludes that there were certainly five thousand, and possibly seven thousand, students at Paris in the early scholastic age, before the multiplication of important centres. He points out that the fabulous figures which are sometimes given—Wycliffe says that at one time there were sixty thousand students at Oxford, Juvenal de Ursinis gives twenty thousand at Paris in the fifteenth century, Italian historians speak of fifteen thousand at Bologna — always refer to a date beyond the writer's experience, and frequently betray a touch of the *laudator temporis acti*. It is, at all events, safe to affirm that Abélard's students were counted by thousands,

if they had not 'come to surpass the number of
the laity' [ordinary citizens], as an old writer
declares. Philippe Auguste had to direct a huge
expansion of the city before the close of the
century. There is nothing in the commercial
or political development of Paris to explain the
magnitude of this expansion. It was a consequence of a vast influx of students from all
quarters of the globe, and the fame of Master
Abélard had determined the course of the
stream.

One condition reacted on another. A notable
gathering of students attracted Jews and merchants
in greater numbers. They, in turn, created innumerable 'wants' amongst the 'undisciplined
horde.' The luxuries and entertainments of
youth began to multiply. The schools of Paris
began to look fair in the eyes of a second world
—a world of youths and men who had not felt
disposed to walk hundreds of miles and endure
a rude life out of academic affection. The
'dancers of Orleans,' the 'tennis-players of
Poitiers,' the 'lovers of Turin,' came to fraternise
with the 'dirty fellows of Paris.' Over mountains and over seas the mingled reputation of the
city and the school was carried, and a remarkable

stream set in from Germany, Switzerland, Italy (even from proud Rome), Spain, and England ; even 'distant Brittany sent you its animals to be instructed,' wrote Prior Fulques to Abélard (a Breton) a year or two afterwards.

At five or six o'clock each morning the great cathedral bell would ring out the summons to work. From the neighbouring houses of the canons, from the cottages of the townsfolk, from the taverns, and hospices, and boarding-houses, the stream of the industrious would pour into the enclosure beside the cathedral. The master's beadle, who levied a precarious tax on the mob, would strew the floor of the lecture-hall with hay or straw, according to the season, bring the Master's text-book, with the notes of the lecture between lines or on the margin, to the solitary desk, and then retire to secure silence in the adjoining street. Sitting on their haunches in the hay, the right knee raised to serve as a desk for the waxed tablets, the scholars would take notes during the long hours of lecture (about six or seven), then hurry home—if they were industrious—to commit them to parchment while the light lasted.

The lectures over, the stream would flow back

over the Little Bridge, filling the taverns and hospices, and pouring out over the great playing meadow, that stretched from the island to the present Champ de Mars. All the games of Europe were exhibited on that international playground : running, jumping, wrestling, hurling, fishing and swimming in the Seine, tossing and thumping the inflated ball—a game on which some minor poet of the day has left us an enthusiastic lyric—and especially the great game of war, in its earlier and less civilised form. The nations were not yet systematically grouped, and long and frequent were the dangerous conflicts. The undergraduate mind, though degrees had not yet been invented, had drawn up an estimate, pithy, pointed, and not flattering, of each nationality. The English were, it is sad to find, 'cowardly and drunken,' —to the 'Anglophobes'; the French were 'proud and effeminate'; the Normans 'charlatans and boasters,' the Burgundians 'brutal and stupid'; the Bretons 'fickle and extravagant'; the Flemings 'blood-thirsty, thievish, and incendiary'; the Germans 'choleric, gluttonous, and dirty'; the Lombards 'covetous, malicious, and no fighters'; the Romans 'seditious, violent, and slanderous.' Once those war-cries were raised, peaceable folk hied them to their homes and hovels, and the governor summoned his guards and archers.

The centre of this huge and novel concourse was the master of the cathedral school. After long years of conventual life Heloise draws a remarkable picture of the attitude of Paris towards its idol. Women ran to their doors and windows to gaze at him, as he passed from his house on St. Genevieve to the school. 'Who was there that did not hasten to observe when you went abroad, and did not follow you with strained neck and staring eyes as you passed along? What wife, what virgin, did not burn? What queen or noble dame did not envy my fortune?' And we shall presently read of a wonderful outburst of grief when the news of the outrage done to Abélard flies through the city. 'No man was ever more loved—and more hated,' says the sober Hausrath.

It is not difficult to understand the charm of Abélard's teaching. Three qualities are assigned to it by the writers of the period, some of whom studied at his feet : clearness, richness in imagery, and lightness of touch are said to have been the chief characteristics of his teaching. Clearness is, indeed, a quality of his written works, though they do not, naturally, convey an impression of his oral power. His splendid gifts and versatility, supported by a rich voice, a charming personality, a ready and sympathetic use of human literature, and a freedom from excessive piety, gave him an immeasurable advantage over all the teachers of the day. Beside most of them, he was as a butterfly to an elephant. A most industrious study of the few works of Aristotle and of the Roman classics that were available, a retentive memory, an ease in manipulating his knowledge, a clear, penetrating mind, with a corresponding clearness of expression, a ready and productive fancy, a great knowledge of men, a warmer interest in things human than in things divine, a laughing contempt for authority, a handsome presence, and a musical delivery—these were his gifts. His only defects were defects of charactcr, and the circumstances of his life had not yet revealed them even to himself.

Even the monkish writers of the *Life of St. Goswin*, whose attitude towards his person is clear, grant him 'a sublime eloquence.' The epitaphs that men raised over him, the judgments of episcopal Otto von Freising and John of Salisbury, the diplomatic letter of Prior Fulques, the references of all the chroniclers of the time, I refrain from quoting. We learn his power best from his open enemies. 'Wizard,' 'rhinoceros,' 'smiter,' 'friend of the devil,' 'giant,' 'Titan,' 'Prometheus,' and 'Proteus,' are a few of their compliments to his ability : the mellifluous St. Bernard alone would provide a rich vocabulary of flattering encomiums of that character : 'Goliath,' 'Herod,' 'Leviathan,' 'bee,' 'serpent,' 'dragon,' 'hydra,' 'Absalom,' are some of his epithets. When, later, we find St. Bernard, the first orator and firmest power in France, shrink nervously from an oral encounter with him, and resort to measures which would be branded as dishonourable in any other man, we shall more faithfully conceive the charm of Abélard's person and the fascination of his lectures.

Yet no careful student of his genius will accept the mediæval estimate which made him the 'Socrates of Gaul,' the peer of Plato and of Aristotle. He had wonderful penetration and a rare felicity of oral expression, but he was far removed from the altitude of Socrates and Plato and the breadth of Aristotle. He had no 'system' of thought, philosophical or theological ; and into the physical and social world he never entered. His ideas—and some of them were leagues beyond his intellectual surroundings— came to him piecemeal. Yet we shall see that in some of those which were most abhorrent to Bernard—who was the Church for the time being —he did but anticipate the judgment of mature humanity on certain ethical and intellectual features of traditional lore. The thesis cannot be satisfactorily established until a later stage.

When we proceed to examine the erudition which gave occasion to the epitaph, 'to him alone was made clear all that is knowable,' we must bear in mind the limitations of his world. When Aristotle lent his mind to the construction of a world system, he had the speculations of two centuries of Greek thinkers before him ; when Thomas of Aquin began to write, he had read the thoughts of three generations of schoolmen after Abélard, and all the Arabic translations and incorporations of Greek thought. At the beginning of the twelfth century there was little to read beside the fathers. If we take 'all that was knowable' in this concrete and relative sense, the high-sounding epitaph is not far above the truth.

His Latin is much better than that of the great majority of his contemporaries. Judged by a per-

fect classical standard it is defective ; it admits
some of the erroneous forms that are characteristic
of the age. But it is not without elegance, and
it excels in clearness and elasticity. It could not
well be otherwise, seeing his wide and familiar
acquaintance with Latin literature. He frequently
quotes Lucan, Ovid, Horace, Vergil, and Cicero ;
students of his writings usually add an acquaintance with Juvenal, Persius, Statius, Suetonius,
Valerius Maximus, Quintilian, and Priscian. It
was a frequent charge in the mouths of his enemies
that he quoted the lewdest books of Ovid in the
course of his interpretation of Scripture. The
constant glance aside at the literature of human
passion and the happy flash of wit were not small
elements in his success. Those who came to him
from other schools had heard little but the wearisome iteration of Boetius, Cassiodorus, and Mar-
tianus Capella. They found the new atmosphere
refreshing and stimulating.

His command of Greek and Hebrew is a subject
of endless dispute. His pupil Heloise certainly
had a knowledge of the two tongues, as we shall
see presently. She must have received her instruction from Abélard. But it is clear that Abélard
likes to approach a controversy which turns on

the interpretation of the original text of Scripture through a third person, such as St. Jerome. He rarely approaches even the easy Greek text of the New Testament directly, and he has no immediate acquaintance with any Greek author. Aristotle he has read in the Latin translation of Boetius, through whose mediation he has also read Porphyry's *Isagoge*. He was certainly familiar with the *De Interpretatione* and the *Categories*; Cousin grants him also an acquaintance with the *Prior Analytics*; and Brucker and others would add the *Sophistici Elenchi* and the *Topics*. The physical and metaphysical works of Aristotle were proscribed at Paris long after the Jewish and Arabian translations had found a way into other schools of France. The golden thoughts of Plato came to him through the writings of the fathers; though there is said to have been a translation of the *Timæus* in France early in the twelfth century.

His knowledge of Hebrew must have been equally, or even more, elementary. Only once does he clearly approach the Hebrew text without patristic guidance; it is when, in answering one (the thirty-sixth) of the famous 'Problems of Heloise,' he adduces the authority of 'a certain Hebrew,' whom he 'heard discussing the point.'

In this we have a clear clue to the source of his Hebrew. The Jews were very numerous in Paris in the twelfth century. When Innocent the Second visited Paris in 1131, the Jews met him at St. Denis, and offered him a valuable roll of the law. By the time of Philippe Auguste they are said to have owned two-thirds of the city : perceiving which, Philippe recollected, or was reminded, that they were the murderers of Christ, and so he banished them and retained their goods. Abélard indicates that they took part in the intellectual life of Paris in his day; in Spain they were distinguished in every branch of higher thought ; and thus the opportunity of learning Hebrew lay close at hand. One does not see why Rémusat and others should deny him any acquaintance with it. His knowledge, however, must have been elementary. He does not make an impressive, though a novel, use of it in deriving the name of Heloise (Helwide, or Helwise, or Louise) from Elohim, which he does, years afterwards, in the sober solitude of his abbey and the coldness of his mutilation.

Add an extensive acquaintance with Scripture and the fathers, and the inventory is complete. Not difficult to be erudite in those days,

most people will reflect. Well, a phonogram
may be erudite. The gifts of Abélard were of a
higher order than industry and memory, though
he possessed both. He takes his place in history,
apart from the ever-interesting drama and the deep
pathos of his life, in virtue of two distinctions.
They are, firstly, an extraordinary ability in im-
parting such knowledge as the poverty of the age
afforded—the facts of his career reveal it ; and
secondly, a mind of such marvellous penetration
that it conceived great truths which it has taken
humanity seven or eight centuries to see—this
will appear as we proceed. It was the former of
these gifts that made him, in literal truth, the
centre of learned and learning Christendom, the
idol of several thousand eager scholars. Nor,
finally, were these thousands the 'horde of barbarians' that jealous Master Roscelin called them.
It has been estimated that a pope, nineteen
cardinals, and more than fifty bishops and archbishops, were at one time among his pupils.

We are now at, or near, the year 1118. In
the thirty-ninth year of his age, the twenty-third
year of his scholastic activity, Abélard has reached
the highest academic position in Christendom.
He who loved so well, and so naturally, to be

admired, found himself the centre of a life that had not been seen since Greek sages poured out wisdom in the painted colonnade, and the marble baths, and the shady groves of Athens. His self-esteem was flattered ; his love of rule and of eminence was gratified. Poor as many of his pupils were, their number brought him great wealth. His refinement had ample means of solacing its desires. The petty vexations of the struggle were nobly compensated. Before him lay a world of fairest promise into which he, seemingly, had but to enter. Then there arose one of the forces that shattered his life, beginning its embodiment in an idyll, ending quickly in a lurid tragedy. It is the most difficult stage in the story of Abélard. I approach it only in the spirit of the artist, pur-posing neither to excuse nor to accuse, but only to trace, if I may, the development of a soul.

Abélard's life had until now been purely spiritual, almost wholly intellectual. His defects were spiritual—conceit and ambition; if, as men assure us, it is a defect to recognise that you have a supra-normal talent, and to strive for the pre-eminence it entitles you to. The idealist spirit in which he had turned away from the comfort and quiet of the château had remained

thus far the one fire that consumed his energy.
In the pretty theory of Plato, his highest soul
had silenced the lower, and reduced the lowest
to the barest requisite play of vegetative life.
There are men who go through life thus. The
scientist would crudely—it is the fashion to say
'crudely'—explain that the supra-normal activity
of the upper part of the nervous system made the
action of the lower part infra-normal; but let us
keep on the spiritual plane. There are men
whose soul is so absorbed in study or in con-
templation that love never reaches their consciousness; or if it does, its appeal is faint, and quickly
rejected. The condition of such a life, highly
prized as it is by many, is constant intellectual
strain.

Abélard had now arrived at a point when
the mental strain began instinctively to relax.
Wealth would inevitably bring more sensuous
pleasure into his life. He was not one of the
'purely intellectual'; he had a warm imagination
and artistic power. No immediate purpose called
for mental concentration. Sensuous enjoyment
crept over the area of his conscious life. During
a large proportion of his time, too, he was following with sympathy the quickening life of the

passionate creations of Ovid and Vergil and
Lucan. The inner judge, the sterner I, is in-
disposed to analyse, unless education, or faith,
or circumstance, has laid a duty of severer watch-
fulness upon it. Blending with other and not
alarming sensuous feelings, veiling itself, and
gently, subtly passing its sweet fire into the veins,
the coming of love is unperceived until it is
already strong to exert a numbing influence on
the mind. Abélard awoke one day to a consciousness that a large part of the new sweetness
that pervaded his life was due to the birth of a
new power in his soul—a power as elusive to
recognition as it is imperious in its demands.
Then is the trial of the soul.

Before quoting Abélard's confession, with
respect to this transformation of his character, it
is necessary, out of justice to him, to anticipate
a little, in indicating the circumstances of the
making of the confession. The long letter which
Abélard entitled the 'Story of my Calamities'
was written twelve or thirteen years after these
events. By that time he had not only endured
a succession of cruel persecutions, but his outlook
on life and on self had been entirely changed.
Not only had the memory of the events faded

F

somewhat, but he had become colour-blind in an important sense. A frightful mutilation had distorted his physical and psychic nature. Partly from this cause, and partly under the stress of other circumstances, he had become a Puritan of the Puritans, an ascetical hermit. As is the wont of such, he manifests a tendency to exaggerate the shadows cast by actions of his which he can no longer understand; for nature has withdrawn her inspiration. On the point we are considering he does not evince the smallest desire of conceal-ment or palliation, but rather the reverse. And, finally, the letter, though written ostensibly for the solace of a friend in distress, was clearly written for circulation, and for the conciliation of the gentler of the Puritans, who knew his life well.

After speaking of the wealth and fame he had attained, he says: 'But since prosperity ever puffs up the fool, and worldly ease dissolves the vigour of the mind, and quickly enervates it by carnal allurements; now that I thought myself to be the only philosopher in the world, and feared no further menace to my position, whereas I had hitherto lived most continently, I began to loose the rein to passion. And the further I had advanced in philosophy and in reading Holy Writ, so much the wider did I depart from philosophers and divines by the uncleanness of my life. It is well known to thee that philosophers and divines have ever been distinguished for this virtue of continence. But, whilst I was thus wholly taken up with pride and lust, the grace of God brought me a remedy, unwilling as I was, for both maladies; for lust first, and then for pride. For lust, by depriving me of its instrument; for pride—the pride which was chiefly born of my knowledge of letters, according to the word of the Apostle, 'knowledge puffeth up'—by humbling me in the burning of the book by which I set such store. And now I would have thee learn the truth of both these stories, from the events themselves rather than from rumour, in the order in which they befell. Since then I had ever abhorred the uncleanness of harlots, and I had been withheld from the company and intercourse of noble dames by the exactions of study, nor had I more than a slight acquaintance with other women, evil fortune, smiling on me, found an easier way to cast me down from the summit of my prosperity; proud, as I was, and unmindful of divine favour, the goodness of God humbled me, and won me to itself.' And the penitent passes on immediately to give the story of his relation to Heloise.

It is quite clear that all the vehement language with which he scourges himself before humanity refers exclusively to his liaison with Heloise. Searching about, as he does, for charges to heap upon his dead self, he yet denies that he had intercourse with women of any description before he knew the one woman whom he loved sincerely throughout life. In a later letter to Heloise, not intended to circulate abroad, he repeats the statement; recalling their embraces, he says they were the more treasured 'since we had never known the like (*ista gaudia*) before.' Moreover, he says a little later in the 'Story' that up to the time of his liaison with Heloise he had a 'repute for chastity' in the city; the events we have to follow prove this to have been the case. Finally, let us carefully remember that there would be no advantage in concealing any earlier disorder, and that there is clear indication, even in the short passage I have quoted, of a disposition rather to magnify faults than to attenuate.

I labour the point, because a writer who has introduced Abélard to many of the present generation, and for whom and whose thoughts I have otherwise a high regard, has somehow been led to lay here a very damning indictment of Abélard. Mr. Cotter Morison was a follower of the religion that worships the departed great, and should have a special care to set in light the character of those whom the Church has bruised in life, and slandered after death, under a false view of the interest of humanity. Yet, in his *Life of St. Bernard*, he has grossly added to the charge against Abélard, with the slenderest of historical bases. It were almost an injustice to Kingsley to say that Cotter Morison's Abélard recalls the great novelist's pitiful Hypatia. The Positivist writer thus interprets this stage in Abélard's career. After saying that his passion broke out like a volcano, and that he felt 'a fierce, fiery thirst for pleasure, sensual and animal,' he goes on in this remarkable strain: 'He drank deeply, wildly. He then grew fastidious and particular. He required some delicacy of romance, some flavour of emotion, to remove the crudity of his lust. He seduced Heloise.'

Was ever a graver perversion in the historical construction of character by an impartial writer? Stranger still, Mr. Cotter Morison has already

warned his readers that the 'Story of my Calamities'
must be shorn of some penitential *exaggeration*, if
we are to give it historical credence.   But Mr.
Morison has witnesses.   Prior Fulques, in a letter
to Abélard, reminded him that he squandered a
fortune on harlots.   The assertion of this monk
of Deuil, based, professedly, on the reports of
Abélard's bitter enemies, the monks of St. Denis,
and made in a letter which is wholly politic, is
held by Mr. Morison to 'more than counterbalance' the solemn public] affirmation of a
morbidly humble, self-accusing penitent.   And
this, after warning us not to take Abélard's self-
accusation too literally!   I shall examine this
letter of Prior Fulques' more closely later.   Not
only does the letter itself belong to, but the
charge refers to, a later period, and will be
weighed then.   There is nothing at this stage to
oppose to the quiet and indirect claim of Abélard,
allowed by the action of Fulbert, that his character was unsullied up to the date of his liaison
with Heloise.

Let us return to the accredited historical facts.
Somewhere about the year 1118 Abélard first felt
the claims of love.   He was wealthy and pro-
sperous, and living in comparative luxury.   He

had those gifts of imagination which usually reveal an ardent temperament. Whether it was Heloise who unwittingly kindled the preparing passion, or whether Abélard yielded first to a vague, imperious craving, and sought one whom he might love, we do not know. But we have his trustworthy declaration that he detested the rampant harlotry, and knew no woman until he felt the sweet caress of Heloise.

I have now to set out with care the story of that immortal love. But nine readers out of ten are minded to pass judgment on the acts and lives of those we recall from the dead. My function is to reconstruct the story as faithfully as the recorded facts allow. Yet I would make one more digression before doing so.

What standard of conduct shall be used in judging Abélard? There are a thousand moral codes — that of the Hindu and that of the Christian, that of the twelfth century and that of the *twentieth*. In the twelfth century even the St. Bernards thought it just that a man who could not see the truth of the Church's claims should be burned alive, and his soul tortured for all eternity ; that a Being was just and adorable who tortured a twelfth century babe for Adam's sin ; that twelfth century Jews might be robbed because their remote ancestors had put Christ to death ; that the sanctity of justice demanded, literally, an eye for an eye ; and so forth. One may, of course, choose whatever standard of conduct one likes to measure Abélard's, or anybody else's, actions : Cardinal Newman, and such writers, have a fancy for judging him by the perfected code of the nineteenth. We cannot quarrel with them ; though it is well to point out that they are not measuring Abélard's subjective guilt, nor portraying his character, in so doing. And if any do elect to judge Abélard by the moral code of the twelfth century, it must be noted that this varied much, even on the point of sexual morality. St. Bernard and his like saw an inherent moral evil in sexual union ; they thought the sanctity of the priestly character was incompatible with it, and that virginity was, in itself, and by the mere abstinence from sexual commerce, something holier than marriage. Apart from this, no doubt—if it can be set apart in the question—good men were agreed. But, as will appear presently, there were large bodies of men, even clerks, who not only differed from them in practice, but also in their deliberate moral judg-

ment. We must approach closer still. When
we have to determine an individual conception
of the law, for the purpose of measuring real and
personal guilt, we must have a regard to the
surrounding influences, the current thoughts and
prevailing habits, which may have impaired or
obscured the feeling of its validity in any respect.
It is well, then, first to glance at the morals of
the time when one feels eager to measure Abélard's guilt.

It was a period when the dark triumph of what
is called materialism, or animalism, was as yet
relieved only by a sporadic gleam of idealism.
There was purity in places, but over the broad
face of the land passion knew little law. If the
unlettered Greek had immoral gods to encourage
him, the mediæval had immoral pastors. The
Church was just endeavouring to enforce its unfortunate law of celibacy on them. With a stroke
of the pen it had converted thousands of honest
wives into concubines. The result was utter and
sad demoralisation. In thus converting the moral
into the deeply immoral, the Church could appeal
to no element in the consciences of its servants ;
nor even to its basic Scriptures. Writers of the
time use hyperbolic language in speaking of the

prevalent vice, and the facts given in the chronicles, and embodied in the modern collections of ancient documents, fully sustain it. Speaking of the close of the eleventh century, Dubois, in his *Historia Ecclesiæ Parisiensis*, says : 'The condition of the Church [in general] at that time was unhappy and wretched . . . nearly all the clergy were infected with the vice of simony . . . lust and shameful pleasure were openly rampant.' It is true that he excepts his 'Church of Paris,' but his own facts show that it is only a piece of foolish loyalty. Cardinal Jacques de Vitry, who studied at Paris towards the close of the century (it must have been worse in Abélard's time), gives a clearly overdrawn, yet instructive, picture of its life in his *Historia Occidentalis*. 'The clergy,' he says, probably meaning the scholars in general, of whom the majority were clerics, 'saw no sin in simple fornication. Common harlots were to be seen dragging off clerics as they passed along to their brothels. If they refused to go, opprobrious names were called after them. School and brothel were under the same roof—the school above, the brothel below . . . And the more freely they spent their money in vice, the more were they commended, and regarded by almost everybody

as fine, liberal fellows.' The vice that has ever
haunted educational centres and institutes was
flagrant and general. It is a fact that the authorities had at length to prohibit the canons to
lodge students in their houses on the island. In
the country and in the other towns the same
conditions were found. In Father Denifle's *Char-
tularium* there is a document (No. v.) which
throws a curious light on the habits of the clergy.
A priest of Rheims was dancing in a tavern one
Sunday, when some of the scholars laughed at
him. He pursued them to their school, took the
place by storm, half-murdered, and then (presumably recalling his sacerdotal character) ex-
communicated them. At another time, Cardinal
Jacques tells us, the lady of a certain manor
warned the priest of the village to dismiss his
concubine. He refused; whereupon the noble
dame had the woman brought to her, and ordained
her 'priestess,' turning her out before the admiring villagers with a gaudy crown. Another poor
priest told his bishop, with many tears, that, if it
were a question of choosing between his church
and his concubine, he should have to abandon the
church; the story runs that, finding his income
gone, the lady also departed. There is an equally

dark lament in Ordericus Vitalis, the Norman, who lived in Abélard's day. The letters and sermons of Abélard—Abélard the monk, of St. Bernard, and of so many others, confirm the darkest features of the picture. Only a few years previously the king had lived with the wife of one of his nobles, in defiance of them all ; and when a council, composed of one hundred and twenty prelates, including two cardinals and a number of bishops, met at Poitiers to censure him, the Duke of Aquitaine broke in with his soldiers, and scattered them with the flat of his sword. Indeed, an ancient writer, Hugo Flaviniacensis, declares there was a feeling that Pope Paschal did not, for financial reasons, approve the censure passed by his legates.

Considering the enormous prevalence of simony, one could hardly expect to find the Church in a better condition. The writers of the time make it clear that there was an appalling traffic in bishoprics, abbeys, prebends, and all kinds of ecclesiastical goods and dignities. We have already seen one tragic illustration of the evil, and we shall meet many more. A few years previously the king had nominated one of his favourites, Étienne de Garlande, for the vacant bishopric of Beauvais ;

and this youth, 'of no letters and of unchaste life,' at once took even major orders, and talked of going to Rome 'to buy the curia.' But, as with regard to the previous point, it is useless to give instances. Corruption was very prevalent; and one cannot wonder at it in view of the reputation which the papacy itself had, in spite of its occasional quashing of a corrupt election. This point will be treated more fully in the sixth chapter.

The question of the deep and widespread corruption of the regular clergy must also be deferred. In his fourth letter to Heloise, Abélard complains that 'almost all the monasteries of our day' are corrupt; Jacques de Vitry affirms that no nunneries, save those of the Cistercians, were fit abodes for an honest woman in his day.[1] It is not a little instructive to find Abbot Abélard, in his latest and most ascetic period, telling his son (a monk), in the course of a number of admirable moral maxims, that : 'A humble harlot is better than she who is chaste and proud,' and that 'Far worse is the shrewd-tongued woman than a harlot.'

Finally, mention must be made of the extreme violence of the age. Several illustrations have

---

[1] The condition of monasteries will be found treated more fully on p. 125; that of nunneries on p. 209.

been given in the course of the narrative, and it
will bring many more before the reader. They
were still the days of the *lex talionis*, the judicial
duel, the ordeal, and the truce of God. Murder
was common in town and country. We have
seen the brutal murder of the Bishop of Laon in
1112 ; we find the Bishop of Paris threatened by
the relatives of his archdeacon, and the Prior of
St. Victor's murdered by them, in 1133. But
the story will contain violence enough. As for
'the undisciplined student-hordes of the Middle
Ages,' see the appalling picture of their life in
Rashdall's *Universities of Europe*. Our period is
pre-university—and worse : with the founding of
the university came some degree of control. Yet
even then the documentary evidence discloses a
fearful condition of violence and lawlessness. In
the year 1197 we find the Bishop of Paris abol-
ishing the 'Feast of Fools.' On January 1st (and
also on the feast of St. Stephen), it seems, a
carnival was held, during which the masquers had
free run of the cathedral and the churches, making
them echo with ribald songs, and profaning them
with bloodshed and all kinds of excess. In 1218,
says Crevier, we find the ecclesiastical judges of
Paris complaining that the students break into the

houses of the citizens, and carry off their women-folk. In 1200 we find a pitched battle between the students of Paris and the governor and his guards, in which several are killed ; and the king condemns the unfortunate governor to be tried by ordeal ; to be hanged forthwith if it proves his guilt, and to be imprisoned for life (in case Providence has made a mistake) if it absolves him. After another of these battles, when the governor has hanged several students, the king forces him and his council to go in their shirts to the scaffold and kiss the bodies. In another case, in 1228, the king sides with the governor, and the masters close the university in disgust until the students are avenged.

But of story-telling there would be no end. And, indeed, there is the danger of giving a false impression of scantiness of evidence when one follows up a large assertion with a few incidents. It is, however, clear from the quoted words of accredited historians, and will be made clearer in the progress of the narrative, that simony, un-chastity, violence, cruelty, and usury were real and broad features of the age of Abélard. The reader will not forget them, when he is seeking to enter into the conscience of the famous master.

CHAPTER V

DEAD SEA FRUIT

THE great cemetery of Père Lachaise at Paris is
a city of historic tombs. Names of world-fame
look down on you from the marble dwellings of
the dead, as you pass along its alleys and broad
avenues. Paris loves to wander there on Sundays ;
to scatter floral symbols of a living memory on
the youngest graves, and to hang wreaths of un-
fading honour over the ashes of those who have
fought for it and served it. The memory of the
dead soon fades, they say, yet you will see men
and women of Paris, on many a summer's day,
take flowers and wreaths in solemn pity to lay on
the tomb of a woman who was dust seven hundred
years ago. It is the grave of Heloise, and of her
lover, Abélard.

It is scarcely necessary to say that in a serious
endeavour to depict the historical Heloise much
myth and legend must be soberly declined.   Even

historians have been seduced from their high duty in writing her praise : witness the fond exaggeration of M. de Rémusat, which would make her 'the first of women.' Yet it must be admitted that impartial study brings us face to face with a very remarkable personality. This will be easily accepted in the sequel, when we have followed the course of her life to some extent—when, for instance, we see the affection and the extraordinary respect with which she inspires the famous abbot of Cluny, Peter the Venerable. It is more difficult to recall her at the period of her fateful meeting with Abélard. We have, however, the sober assurance of Peter the Venerable that, even at this early date, she was ' of great repute throughout the entire kingdom ' ; and there is no reason whatever to resent Abélard's assertion that she was already distinguished for her knowledge.

The mythic additions to the portraiture of Heloise refer almost exclusively to her parentage and her beauty. Abélard introduces her to us as the niece of a canon of the cathedral chapter, named Fulbert. It is quite clear that Abélard considered her such throughout life, and that it was the belief of Heloise herself ; but of her parentage neither of them speaks. In strict

G

justice, the only inference we may draw from this is that she lost her parents at an early age. We should never have known the parentage of Abélard but for his own autobiography. However, the tradition that has charged itself with the romance of Abélard's life found in this silence a convenient pretext for weaving further romantic elements into the story. There is a pretty collection of myths about Heloise's birth, most of them, of course, making her illegitimate. The issue of lawful wedlock is ever too prosaic and ordinary for the romantic faculty—in spite of facts. The favourite theory is that Heloise was the daughter of Canon Fulbert; even Hausrath thinks Fulbert's conduct points to this relationship. Two other canons of Paris are severally awarded the honour by various writers. On the other hand, it was inevitable that she should be given a tinge of 'noble' blood, and this is traced on the maternal side. Turlot makes the best effort— from the romantic point of view—in describing her as the daughter of an abbess, who was the mistress of a Montmorency, but who gave an air of respectability to her family matters by passing for the mistress of Fulbert. From the less interesting point of view of history, we can only say that she lived with her uncle, Canon Fulbert, and we must admit that we do not know whether she was illegitimate or an orphan. But the former category was very much the larger one, even in those violent days.

It was also natural that tradition should endow her with a singular beauty : an endowment which sober history is unable to confirm. She must, it is true, have had a singular grace and charm of person. It is impossible to think that her mental gifts alone attracted Abélard. Moreover, in the course of the story, we shall meet several instances of the exercise of such personal power. But we cannot claim for her more than a moderate degree of beauty. 'Not the least in beauty of countenance,' says Abélard, 'she was supreme in her knowledge of letters.' The antithesis does not seem to be interpreted aright by those writers who think it denies her any beauty. 'Not the least' is a figure of rhetoric, well known to Abélard, which must by no means be taken with Teutonic literalness.

But that 'repute throughout the kingdom,' which Peter the Venerable grants her, was based on her precocious knowledge. It is generally estimated that she was in her seventeenth or

eighteenth year when Abélard fell in love with
her.   She had spent her early years at the Benedictine nunnery at Argenteuil, a few miles beyond
St. Denis.   Her education was then continued by
her uncle.   Canon Fulbert has no reputation for
learning in the chronicles of the time ; in fact,
the only information we have of him, from other
sources than the story of Abélard, is that he was
the happy possessor of ' a whole bone ' out of the
spine of St. Ebrulfus.   However, it is indisputable
that Heloise had a reputation for letters even at
that time.   Both Abélard and Peter of Cluny are
explicit on the point ; the latter says to her, in
one of his admiring letters, 'in study you not
only outstripped all women, but there were few
men whom you did not surpass.'   From this it is
clear that the learning of Heloise was not distinguished only when compared with the general
condition of the feminine mind.   In fact, although
Abbot Peter speaks slightingly of womanly education in general, this was a relatively bright
period.   We have already seen the wife and
daughters of Manegold teaching philosophy at
Paris with much distinction at the close of the
eleventh century, and one cannot go far in the
chronicles of the time without meeting many

instances of a learned correspondence in Latin between prelates and women.

Nevertheless, the learning of Heloise cannot have been considerable, absolutely speaking. Her opportunities were even more limited than the erudition of her time. That she knew Hebrew is explicitly stated by Abélard and Peter of Cluny, and also by Robert of Auxerre ; but she probably learned it (with Greek) from Abélard, and knew no more than he. Her Latin is good ; but it is impossible to discuss here her famous *Letters*, which give us our sole direct insight into her personality. Learned, critical, penetrative, she certainly was, but Rémusat's estimate is entirely inadmissible. Beside Aspasia or Hypatia she would 'pale her ineffectual fire.'

It is not difficult to understand how the two were brought together. Both of high repute 'in the whole kingdom,' or, at all events, in Paris, they could not long remain strangers. Abélard was soon 'wholly afire with love of the maid,' he tells us, and sought an opportunity of closer intercourse with her. Though Cotter Morison's theory of the sated sensualist looking round for a dainty morsel is utterly at variance with Abélard's narrative—the only account of these events that we have—it is, nevertheless, clear that Abélard sought the intimacy of Heloise for the purpose of gaining her love. He says so repeatedly ; and, though we have at times to moderate the stress of his words, we cannot refuse to accept their substance. Mr. Poole considers the idea of a deliberate seduction on the part of Abélard 'incredible.' It is strange that one who is so familiar with the times should think this. 'I thought it would be well to contract a union of love with the maid,' Abélard says. From the circumstance that he had to approach Fulbert (who was, however, only too willing) through the mediation of friends, it does not seem rash to infer that he had had no personal intercourse with the canon and his niece. It was through her fame and, perhaps, an occasional passing glance that he had come to love her. He had, however, little diffidence about the issue. Though between thirty-five and forty years of age, he looked ' young and handsome,' he tells us ; and we learn further from Heloise that he had gifts 'of writing poetry and of singing' which no female heart could resist. The 'Socrates of Gaul' set out on a love-adventure.

And one fine day the little world of Paris was smirking and chattering over the startling news that Master Peter had gone to live with Heloise and her uncle. The simple canon had been delighted at the proposal to receive Abélard. Alleging the expense of maintaining a separate house and the greater convenience of Fulbert's house for attending the school, Abélard had asked his hospitality in consideration of a certain payment and the instruction of Heloise in leisure hours. It may or may not be true that Fulbert was avaricious, as Abélard affirms, but the honour of lodging the first master in Christendom and the valuable advantage to his niece are quite adequate to explain Fulbert's eager acceptance. 'Affection for his niece and the repute of my chastity,' says Abélard, blinded the canon to the obvious danger, if not the explicit intention. The master was at once established in the canon's house. One reads with pity how the uncle, blind, as only an erudite priest can be, to the rounded form and quickened pulse, child-like, gave Abélard even power to beat his niece, if she neglected her task.

A tradition, which seems to have but a precarious claim to credence, points out the spot where the idyll of that love was lived. In the earlier part of the present century there was a

house at the corner of the Rue des Chantres (on
the island, facing the Hotel de Ville), which bore
an inscription claiming that 'Heloise and Abélard,
the model of faithful spouses, dwelt in this house.'
If we accept the vague legend, we can easily
restore in imagination the little cottage of Fulbert.
It lay a few yards from the water's edge, and one
could look out from its narrow windows over the
gently sloping garden of the bank and the fresh,
sweet bosom of the river; the quays were beyond
—where the Hotel de Ville now stands—and
further still outspread the lovely panorama that
encircled Paris.

In a very short time master and pupil were
lovers. He did assuredly fulfil his promise of
teaching her. Most probably it was from him
that she learned what Greek and Hebrew she
knew; for Abélard, in later years, not only
reminds her nuns that they 'have a mother who
is conversant with these tongues,' but adds also
that 'she alone has attained this knowledge,'
amongst the women of her time. It is also clear
that he taught her dialectics, theology, and ethics.
But it was not long, he confesses, before there
were 'more kisses than theses,' and 'love was
the inspirer of his tongue.' He does not hesitate

to speak of having 'corrupted' or seduced her, but it is only prejudice or ignorance that can accept this in the full severity and gravity of the modern term.   Heloise had been educated in a nunnery ; but before many years we find these nuns of Argenteuil turned on the street for 'the enormity of their lives.'   The charge must not be taken too literally just yet, but it should make us hesitate to credit Heloise with a rigorous moral education. She lived, too, in a world where, as we saw, such liaisons were not considered sinful.   It is far from likely that she would oppose any scruple to Abélard's desire.   Indeed, from the study of her references to their love, in the letters she wrote long years afterwards— wrote as an abbess of high repute—one feels disposed to think that Abélard would have had extreme difficulty in pointing out to her the sinfulness of such a love.   It is with an effort, even after twenty years of chaste, conventual life, that she accepts the ecclesiastical view of their conduct.   Abélard sinned ; but let us, in justice, limit his sin at least to its due objective proportion ; its subjective magnitude I shall not venture to examine.

In a few months the famed philosopher appeared in a new character, as 'the first of the troubadours,' to use the words of Ampère. 'À mesure qu'on a plus d'esprit les passions sont plus grandes,' said Pascal. Of all false epigrams that is surely the falsest, but it would be easily inspired by the transformation of Pierre Abélard. The sober-living man of forty, whom all had thought either never to have known or long since to have passed the fever of youth, was mastered by a deep, tyrannical passion. The problems of dialectics were forgotten, the alluring difficulties of Ezechiel unheeded. Day after day the murmuring throng was dismissed untaught from the cloistral school ; whilst passers-by heard songs that were ardent with deep love from the windows of the canon's house. All Paris, even all France, caught the echo, says Heloise, and 'every street, every house, resounded with my name.' The strange 'Story of love and learning,' as an old ballad expressed it, was borne through the kingdom in Abélard's own impassioned words.[1]

Months ran on, and the purblind priest re-

[1] Not a single one of Abélard's songs has come down to us. A few songs are to be found which bear his name, but they are not genuine. It is an unfortunate loss, since the religious hymns of his later years convey no better impression of his true and unspoiled poetic faculty than the moonlight does of the rays of the sun.

mained wholly unconscious of what all Paris sang
nightly in its taverns. At length the truth was
forced upon his mind, and he at once interrupted
the love-story. He drove Abélard from the
house, and raised the usual futile barriers to the
torrent of passion. Whether the canon was really
more earnest than the majority of his order, and
therefore sincerely shocked at the thought of the
liaison, or whether it had disturbed some other
project he had formed, it is impossible to say.
Heloise herself, in her sober maturity, affirms
that any woman in France would have thought
her position more honourable than any marriage.
However that may be, Fulbert angrily forbade a
continuance of the relation. Once more Abélard
must have felt the true alternative that honour
placed before him : either to crush his passion
and return to the school, or to marry Heloise
and sacrifice the desire of further advancement
in ecclesiastical dignity.

Abélard was not a priest at that time. He
was probably a canon of Notre Dame, but there
are very satisfactory reasons for holding that he
did not receive the priesthood until a much later
date. In the 'Story' he makes Heloise address
him, about this time, as 'a cleric and canon,' but

he is nowhere spoken of as a priest. Had he
been a priest, the circumstance would have afforded
Heloise one of the most powerful objections to
a marriage; in the curious and lengthy catalogue
of such objections which we shall find her raising
presently she does not mention the priesthood.
But even if he were a priest, it is not at all clear
that he would have considered this in itself an
impediment to marriage. From the acts of the
Council of London (1102), the Council of Troyes
(1107), the Council of Rheims (1119), and others,
we find that the decree of the Church against the
marriage of priests, and even bishops, was far
from being universally accepted. Indeed, we
have specific reason for thinking that Abélard
did not recognise an impediment of that character.
In a work which bears the title *Sententiae Abaelardi*,
we find the thesis, more or less clearly stated, that
the priest may marry. The work is certainly
not Abélard's own composition, but the experts
regard it as a careful summary of his views by
some master of the period.

Apart from the laxer view of love-relation
which Abélard probably shared, we can only find
firm ground to interpret his reluctance to marry
in the fear of injuring his further ambition.

Marriage was fast becoming a fatal obstacle to advancement in the ecclesiastical world ; a lover— with wealth—was not a serious difficulty.   Even this point, however, cannot be pressed ; it looks as though his ambition had become as limp and powerless as all other feelings in the new tyranny of love.   Historians have been so eager to quarrel with the man that they have, perhaps, not paid a just regard to the fact that Heloise herself was violently opposed to marriage, and conscientiously thought their earlier union more honourable. This will appear presently.

Whatever struggle may have distracted Abélard after their separation, he was soon forced to take practical measures.   Heloise found means to inform him—not with the conventional tears, but, he says, 'with the keenest joy'—that she was about to become a mother.   Fate had cut the ethical knot.   He at once removed her from Fulbert's house during the night, and had her conveyed, in the disguise of a nun,[1] to his home at Pallet.   It is not clearly stated that Abélard accompanied her, but, beside the intrinsic proba-

[1] This detail is round in Abélard's second letter to Heloise. It is characteristic of Mr. Cotter Morison's 'sketch' of Abélard that he should have missed it, and thought fit to deny it.   Deutsch reads him a severe lesson on the duty of accuracy in his *Peter Abälard*.

bility, there is a local tradition that Abélard and Heloise spent many happy months together at Pallet, and there is a phrase in the 'Story' which seems to confirm it. However that may be, we find him in Paris again, after a time, seeking a reconciliation with Fulbert.

Fulbert was by no means the quiet, passive recluse that one would imagine from his earlier action, or inaction. The discovery of Abélard's treachery and the removal of his niece had enkindled thoughts of wild and dark revenge. He feared, however, to attack Abélard whilst Heloise remained at Pallet; it is a fearful commentary on the times that Abélard should coolly remark that a retaliation on the part of his own relatives was apprehended. Revenge was considered a legitimate daughter of justice in those days. A compromise was at length imagined by Abélard. He proposed to marry Heloise, if Fulbert and his friends would agree to keep the marriage secret. In this we have a still clearer revelation of the one serious flaw in Abélard's character— weakness. No doubt, if we had had an autobiography from an unmaimed Abélard—an Abélard who identified himself with, and endeavoured proudly to excuse, the lover of Heloise—we

should be reminded of many extenuating elements ; the repugnance of Heloise, the stupid
anti-matrimonialism of the hierarchy, the current
estimate of an unconsecrated liaison, and so forth.
Even as it is, Abélard perceives no selfishness,
no want of resolution, in his action. ' Out of
compassion for his great anxiety,' he says, he
approached Fulbert on the question of a private
marriage. The canon consented, though secretly
retaining his intention of taking a bloody revenge,
Abélard thinks ; and the master hastened once
more to Brittany for his bride.

Abélard probably flattered himself that he had
found an admirable outlet from his narrow
circumstances. Fulbert's conscience would be
salved by the Church's blessing on their love ;
the hierarchy would have no matrimonial impediment to oppose to his advancement ; Paris would
give an indulgent eye to what it would regard
as an amiable frailty, if not a grace of character.
Unfortunately for his peace, Heloise energetically
repulsed the idea of marriage. The long passage
in which Abélard gives us her objections is not
the least interesting in the ' Story.'

' She asked,' he writes, ' what glory she would
win from me, when she had rendered me in-

glorious, and had humbled both me and her.
How great a punishment the world would inflict
on her if she deprived it of so resplendent a light:
what curses, what loss to the Church, what philosophic tears, would follow such a marriage. How
outrageous, how pitiful it was, that he whom
nature had created for the common blessing
should be devoted to one woman, and plunged
in so deep a disgrace. Profoundly did she hate
the thought of a marriage which would prove so
humiliating and so burdensome to me in every
respect.'

Then follows an elaborate, rhetorical discourse
on the disadvantages of matrimony, with careful
division and subdivision, arguments from reason,
from experience, from authority, and all the
artifices of rhetoric and dialectics. That the
learned Heloise did urge many of its curious
points will scarcely be doubted, but as a careful
and ordered piece of pleading against matrimony
it has an obvious ulterior purpose. St. Paul is
the first authority quoted ; then follow St. Jerome,
Theophrastus, and Cicero. She (or he) then
draws an animated picture of the domestic felicity
of a philosopher, reminding him of servants and
cradles, infant music and the chatter of nurses,

the pressing throng of the family and the helplessness of the little ones. The example of monks, of Nazarites, and of philosophers is impressively urged ; and if he will not hesitate, as 'a cleric and a canon,' to commit himself 'irrevocably to domestic joy,' at least let him remember his dignity as a philosopher. The sad fate of the married Socrates is adduced, together with the thunder and rain incident. Finally, she is represented as saying that it is 'sweeter to her and more honourable to him that she should be his mistress rather than his wife,' and that she prefers to be united to him 'by love alone, not by the compulsion of the marriage vow.'

When the letter containing this curious passage reached Heloise, nearly twenty years after the event, she, an abbess of high repute for holiness, admitted its correctness, with the exception that 'a few arguments had been omitted in which she set love before matrimony and freedom before compulsion.' Holy abbess writing to holy abbot, she calls God to witness that 'if the name of wife is holier, the name of friend, or, if he likes, mistress or concubine, is sweeter,' and that she 'would rather be his mistress than the queen of a Cæsar.' They who disregard these things in sitting in judgment on that famous liaison are foredoomed to error.

But Abélard prevailed. 'Weeping and sobbing vehemently,' he says, 'she brought her discourse to an end with these words : "One thing alone remains for us now, we must exhibit in our common ruin a grief as strong as the love that has gone before."' It is an artistic termination to Abélard's discourse, at all events.

Back to Paris once more, therefore, the two proceeded. Heloise had a strong foreboding of evil to come from the side of Fulbert ; she did not trust his profession of conciliation. However, she left her boy, whom, with a curious affectation, they had called Astrolabe (the name of an astronomic apparatus), in the charge of Abélard's sister Denyse. They were married a few days after their arrival at Paris. The vigil was spent, according to custom, in one of the churches : they remained all night in prayer, and the ceremony took place after an early Mass in the morning. Their arrival in Paris had been kept secret, and only Fulbert and a few friends of both parties were present at the marriage. Then they parted at the altar : the man weakly proceeding to follow his poor ambition in the school, the noble young wife making herself a sad sacrifice to his selfishness and irresolution.

During the next few dreary months they saw each other rarely and in secret. Abélard was a man of the type that waits for the compulsion of events in a serious conflict of desires, or of desire and duty. He could not lay aside his day-dream that somehow and some day the fates would smooth out a path along which he could carry both his whole ambition and his love. Events did decide for him once more. Fulbert, it seems, broke his faith with Abélard and divulged the marriage. But when people came to Heloise for confirmation, she did more than ' lie with the sweetness of a Madonna,' in Charles Reade's approving phrase ; she denied on oath that she was the wife of Abélard. Fulbert then began to ill-treat her (the circumstance may be commended to the notice of those historians who think he had acted from pure affection), and Abélard removed her secretly from her uncle's house.

It was to the convent at Argenteuil that Abélard conveyed his wife this time. One passes almost the very spot in entering modern Paris by the western line, but the village lay at a much greater distance from the ancient island-city, a few miles beyond St. Denis, going down the river. It was a convent of Benedictine nuns, very familiar to Heloise, who had received her early education there. In order to conceal Heloise more effectually, he bade her put on the habit of the nuns, with the exception of the veil, which was the distinguishing mark of the professed religious. Here she remained for some months; Abélard waiting upon events, as usual, and occasionally making a secret visit to Argenteuil. According to Turlot, the abbess of Argenteuil was the mother of Heloise. We know, at least, that the nunnery was in a very lax condition, and that, beyond her unconquerable presentiment of evil, Heloise would suffer little restraint. Indeed, Abélard reminds her later, in his second letter to her, that their conjugal relations continued whilst she was in the nunnery.

How long this wretched situation continued it is impossible to determine. It cannot have been many months, at the most, before Fulbert discovered what had happened; it was probably a matter of weeks. Yet this is the only period in which it is possible to entertain the theory of Abélard's licentiousness. We have already seen that Cotter Morison's notion of a licentious

period before the liaison with Heloise is quite
indefensible. The tragic event which we have
presently to relate puts the latest term to the
possibility of such licence. Now, there are two
documents on which Abélard's critics rely : a
letter to him from Fulques, prior in the monastery
of Deuil near Paris, and a letter from his former
teacher, Master Roscelin. Prior Fulques, however, merely says he 'has heard' that Abélard
was reduced to poverty through 'the greed and
avarice of harlots' ; and Roscelin explicitly states
that he heard his story from the monks of St.
Denis. Indeed, we may at once exclude Roscelin's
letter ; not merely because it was written in a
most furious outburst of temper, when a man
would grasp any rumour, but also on the ground
that his story is absurd and impossible. He
represents Abélard, when a monk at St. Denis,
later, returning to his monastery with the money
earned by his teaching, and marching off with it
to pay a former mistress. We shall see, in a
later chapter, that Abélard did not begin to teach
until he had left St. Denis.

If, however, Roscelin's story is too absurd to
entertain in itself, it is useful in casting some
light on Fulques's letter. Fulques was writing to

Abélard on behalf of the monks of St. Denis. He would be well acquainted with their gossip, and would, therefore, probably be referring to the story which Roscelin shows to be impossible in giving it more fully. It is not unlikely that the story was really a perverse account of Abélard's visits to Heloise at Argenteuil. In any case we are reduced to the gossip of a band of monks of notorious character (*teste* St. Bernard), of indirect and uncertain information, and of bitter hostility to Abélard.

And this is all the evidence which can be found in support of the calumny. On the strength of this monkish gossip we are asked to believe that Abélard grossly deceived his young wife, and made an attempt, as ridiculous (if the rumour contained truth) as it was hypocritical, to deceive the readers of his heart-naked confession. We are to suppose that 'the abhorrence of harlots,' of which he spoke earlier, entirely disappeared when he found himself united by the sacred bonds of both religion and love to a noble and devoted wife. We are to suppose that his apparent detestation and condemnation of his past conduct was a mere rhetorical artifice to conceal the foulest and most extraordinary episode in his career from the people amongst whom he had lived—an artifice, more-ever, which would be utterly inconsistent with his life and character at the time he wrote the 'Story.' It is almost impossible to take such a notion seriously.

Once more, then, we are in a period of waiting for the direction of events. It came this time in tragic accents that for ever cured the unfortunate Breton of his listless trust in fate.

Fulbert learned at length that Heloise had been sent to Argenteuil, and had taken the habit. The canon at once inferred that this was a preliminary step to a dissolution of the marriage. He would be unaware that it had been consummated, and would suppose that Abélard intended to apply to Rome for a dispensation to relieve him of an apparent embarrassment. He decided on a fearful revenge, which should at least prevent Abélard from marrying another.

And one early morning, a little later, Paris was in a frenzy of excitement. Canons, students, and citizens, thronged the streets, and pressed towards Abélard's house on St. Genevieve. 'Almost the entire city,' says Fulques, went clamouring towards his house : 'women wept as though each one had lost her husband.' Abélard had been brutally mutilated during the night. Hirelings of Canon Fulbert had corrupted his valet, and entered his room whilst he slept. They had perpetrated an indescribable outrage, such as was not infrequently inflicted in the quarrels of the Patareni and the Nicolaitæ. In that dark night the sunshine disappeared for ever from the life of Pierre Abélard. Henceforth we have to deal with a new man.

It is a pious theory of the autobiographist himself that this mutilation led indirectly to his 'conversion.' There is undoubtedly much truth in this notion of an indirect occasioning of better thoughts and of an indirect influence being cast on his mind for life. Yet we of the later date, holding a truer view of the unity of human nature, and of the place that sex-influence occupies in its life, can see that the 'conversion' was largely a direct, physical process. We have, in a very literal sense, another man to deal with henceforward.

As Abélard lay on the bed of sickness, the conversion gradually worked onwards towards a critical decision. It is not clear that the mutilation would prove of itself an impediment to scholastic honour or ecclesiastical office, but the old life could not be faced again by one with so little strength and so keen a sensibility. 'I

pondered on the glory I had won and on the
swift chance blow that had obscured it, nay,
wholly extinguished it: on the just judgment of
God by which I had been punished in the member
that had sinned : on the justice of treachery
coming from him whom I had myself betrayed :
on the joy of my rivals at such a humiliation : on
the endless sorrow this wound would inflict on
my family and my friends : on the speed with
which this deep disgrace would travel through the
world.   What path was open to me now ?   How
could I ever walk abroad again, to be pointed at
by every finger, ridiculed by every tongue, a
monstrous spectacle to all? . . . In such sorry
plight as I was, the confusion of shame rather
than a devout conversion impelled me to seek
refuge in the monastery.'

To this natural 'confusion of shame' we must
look for an explanation of, not merely the folly,
but the cruelty and selfishness, of Abélard's proposal.   It involved the burial of Heloise in a
nunnery.   No one could shrink more feelingly
from the unnatural shade of the cloister than did
Heloise, as Abélard must have known, but in his
pain and despair he forgot the elementary dictates
of love or of honour.   In any other circumstances

the act would be deemed brutal. Indeed, he wantonly increased the suffering of his young wife by ordering her to take the vows first. Twenty years afterwards she plaintively tells him the sorrow he gave her by such a command. 'God knows,' she says, 'I should not have hesitated, at your command, to precede or to follow you to hell itself.' She was 'profoundly grieved and ashamed' at the distrust which seemed to be implied in his direction. But hers was the love that 'is stronger than death,' and she complied without a murmur, making of her sunny nature one more victim on the altar of masculine selfishness.

Abélard has left us a dramatic picture of her taking the vows. It shows clearly that the love which impelled her to such a sacrifice was not the blind, child-like affection that is wholly merged in the stronger loved one, but the deep, true love that sees the full extent of the sacrifice demanded, and accepts it with wide-opened eyes. At the last moment a little group of friends surrounded her in the convent-chapel. The veil, blessed by the bishop, lay on the altar before them, and they were endeavouring to dissuade her from going forward to take it. She waved them aside— waved aside for the last time the thought of her

child and the vision of a sun-lit earth—and took
the fateful step towards the altar. Then, standing on the spot where the young nun generally
knelt for the final thanksgiving to God, she
recited with the tense fervour of a human prayer
the words of Cornelia in Lucan :

> ' O spouse most great,
> O thou whose bed my merit could not share !
> How hath an evil fortune worked this wrong
> On thy dear head ?   Why hapless did I wed,
> If this the fruit that my affection bore ?
> Behold the penalty I now embrace
> For thy sweet sake ! '

And, weeping and sobbing, she walked quickly
up the steps of the altar, and covered herself with
the veil of the religious profession.

CHAPTER VI

THE MONK OF ST. DENIS

ABÉLARD had now entered upon the series of blunders which were to make his life a succession of catastrophes. A stronger man would have retired to Pallet, and remained there until the discussion of his outrage had abated somewhat ; then boldly, and, most probably, with complete success, have confronted the scholastic world once more, with his wife for fitting companion, like Manegold of Alsace. In his distraction and abnormal sense of humiliation, Abélard grasped the plausible promise of the monastic life. In the second place, he, with a peculiar blindness, chose the abbey of St. Denis for his home.

The abbey of St. Denis was not only one of the most famous monasteries in Europe, but also a semi-religious, semi-secular monarchical institution. It was the last monastery in the world to provide that quiet seclusion which Abélard sought.

It lay about six miles from Paris, near one of the many bends of the Seine on its journey to the sea.   Dagobert was its royal founder ; its church was built over the alleged bones of the alleged St. Denis the Areopagite, the patron of France ; it was the burial-place of the royal house.   Over its altar hung the oriflamme of St. Denis, the palladium of the country, which the king came to seek, with solemn rite and procession, whenever the cry of 'St. Denis for France' rang through the kingdom.   Amongst its several hundred monks were the physicians and the tutors of kings —Prince Louis of France was even then studying in its school.

Rangeard, in his history of Brittany, says, that at the beginning of the twelfth century there were more irregular than regular abbeys in France. Abélard himself writes that ' nearly all the monasteries' of his time were worldly.   The truth is that few monasteries, beside those which had been very recently reformed, led a very edifying life.   Hence it is not surprising, when one regards the secular associations of the place, to find that the Benedictine abbey of St. Denis was in a very lax condition.   Abélard soon discovered that, as he says, it was an abbey ' of very worldly

and most disgraceful life.' The great rhetorician
has a weakness for the use of superlatives, but
other witnesses are available. St. Bernard wrote
of it, in his famed, mellifluous manner, that it was
certain the monks gave to Cæsar the things that
were Cæsar's, but doubtful if they gave to God
the things that were God's. A chronicler of the
following century, Guillaume de Nangis, writes
that 'the monks scarcely exhibited even the
appearance of religion.'

The abbey had not been reformed since 994,
so that human nature had had a considerable
period in which to assert itself. The preceding
abbot, Ives I., was accused at Rome of having
bought his dignity in a flagrant manner. The
actual abbot, Adam, is said by Abélard to have
been 'as much worse in manner of life and more
notorious than the rest as he preceded them in
dignity.' It is certainly significant that the Benedictine historian of the abbey, Dom Felibien, can
find nothing to put to the credit of Adam, in
face of Abélard's charge, except a certain generos-
ity to the poor. Nor have later apologists for the
angels, de Nangis, Duchesne, etc., been more
successful. Ecclesiastical history only finds consolation in the fact that Adam's successor was

converted by Bernard in 1127, and at once set about the reform of the abbey.

When Abélard donned the black tunic of the Benedictine monk in it, probably in 1119, the royal abbey was at the height of its gay career. St. Bernard himself gives a bright picture of its life in one of his letters. He speaks of the soldiers who thronged its cloisters, the jests and songs that echoed from its vaulted roofs, the women who contributed to its gaiety occasionally. From frequent passages in Abélard we learn that the monks often held high festival. It may be noted that monastic authorities nearly always give occasion to these festivities, for, even in the severest rules, one always finds an egg, or some other unwonted luxury, admitted on 'feast-days.' It is the consecration of a principle that no body of men and women on earth can apply and appreciate better than monks and nuns. The feasts of St. Denis rivalled those of any château in gay France. The monks were skilful at mixing wine —it is a well-preserved monastic tradition—their farmer-vassals supplied food of the best in abundance, and they hired plenty of conjurors, singers, dancers, jesters, etc., to aid the task of digestion.

Nor was the daily life too dull and burdensome.

Royal councils were frequently held at the abbey, and one does not need much acquaintance with monastic life to appreciate that circumstance. Then there was the school of the abbey, with its kingly and noble pupils—and corresponding visitors : there was the continual stream of interesting guests to this wealthiest and most famous of all abbeys : there was the town of St. Denis, which was so intimately dependent on the abbey. Above all, there were the country-houses, of which the abbey had a large number, and from which it obtained a good deal of its income. Some dying sinner would endeavour to corrupt the Supreme Judge by handing over a farm or a château, with its cattle, and men and women, and other commodities of value, to the monks of the great abbey. These would be turned into snug little 'cells' or 'priories,' and important sources of revenue. Sometimes, too, they had to be fought for in the courts, if not by force of arms. Abélard complains that 'we [monks] compel our servants to fight duels for us' : he has already complained of the frequent presentation to monasteries of both man and maid servants. In 1111 we find some of the monks of St. Denis, at the head of a small army, besieging the chateau of Puiset, capturing its lieutenant, and casting him into a monastic prison. At Toury Abbot Adam had his important dependence armed as a fortress, and made a financial speculation in the opening of a public market. Rangeard tells us, in addition, that many of the monks were expert in canon law, and they travelled a good deal, journeying frequently to Rome in connection with matrimonial and other suits.

But before Abélard turned his attention to the condition of the abbey, he was long preoccupied with the thought of revenge. Revenge was a branch virtue of justice in those days, and Abélard duly demanded the punishment of *talio*. The valet, who had betrayed him, and one of the mutilators, had been captured, and had lost their eyes, in addition to suffering the same mutilation as they had inflicted. But Abélard seems to have been painfully insistent on the punishment of Fulbert. The matter belonged to the spiritual court, since Abélard was a cleric, and Bishop Girbert does not seem to have moved quickly enough for the new monk. Fulbert escaped from Paris, and all his goods were confiscated, but this did not meet Abélard's (and the current) idea of justice. He began to talk of an appeal to Rome.

In these circumstances was written the famous

I

letter of Prior Fulques, to which we have referred
more than once. It is a characteristic piece of
mediæval diplomacy. Fulques was the prior of
Deuil, in the valley of Montmorency, a dependency
of the abbey of St. Florent de Saumur. He was
apparently requested by the abbot of St. Denis to
persuade Abélard to let the matter rest. At all
events, he begins his letter with a rhetorical
description of Abélard's success as a teacher,
depicting Britons and Italians and Spaniards
braving the terrors of the sea, the Alps, and
the Pyrenees, under the fascination of Abélard's
repute. Then, with a view to dissuading him from
the threatened appeal to Rome, he reminds him
of his destitution and of the notorious avarice of
Rome. There is no reason why we should hesitate
to accept Fulques's assertion that Abélard had no
wealth to offer the abbey when he entered it. If,
as seems to be the more correct proceeding, we
follow the opinion that he spent the interval
between the first withdrawal of Heloise and the
marriage with her at Pallet, he cannot have earned
much during the preceding two or three years.
He was hardly likely to be a provident and
economical person. Most of whatever money he
earned, after he first began to serve up stale dishes

to his students in the absorption of his passion, would probably pass into the coffers of Fulbert or, later, of the nunnery at Argenteuil. There is no need whatever to entertain theories of licentiousness from that ground. We have, moreover, already sufficiently discussed that portion of Fulques's letter.

But the second part of the prior's argument, the avarice of Rome, requires a word of comment. It is characteristic of the ecclesiastical historian that in Migne's version of Fulques's letter the indictment of Abélard is given without comment, and the indictment of Rome is unblushingly omitted. It might be retorted that such historians as Deutsch and Hausrath insert the indictment against Rome, and make a thousand apologies for inserting the charge against Abélard. The retort would be entirely without sting, since a mass of independent evidence sustains the one charge, whilst the other is at variance with evidence. The passage omitted in Migne, which refers to Abélard's proposal to appeal to Rome, runs as follows. ' O pitiful and wholly useless proposal ! Hast thou never heard of the avarice and the impurity of Rome ? Who is wealthy enough to satisfy that devouring whirl-pool of harlotry ? Who would ever be able to

fill their avaricious purses? Thy resources are
entirely insufficient for a visit to the Roman
Pontiff. . . . For all those who have approached
that see in our time without a weight of gold
have lost their cause, and have returned in confusion and disgrace.'

Let us, in justice, make some allowance for the
exigency of diplomacy and the purposes of rhetoric ;
the substance of the charge is abundantly supported
by other passages in Migne's own columns.   For
instance, Abbot Suger, in his *Vita Ludovici Grossi*,
says of his departure from Rome after a certain
mission, 'evading the avarice of the Romans we
took our leave.'   The same abbot speaks of their
astonishment at St. Denis when Paschal ii. visited
the abbey in 1106 : 'contrary to the custom of
the Romans, he not only expressed no affection
for the gold, silver, and precious pearls of the
monastery (about which much fear had been entertained),' but did not even look at them.   It
may be noted, without prejudice, that Paschal was
seeking the sympathy and aid of France in his
quarrel with Germany.   In the apology of Beren-
garius, which is also found in Migne, there is
mention of 'a Roman who had learned to love
gold, rather than God, in the Roman curia.'

Bernard of Cluny, a more respectable witness, tersely informs us that 'Rome gives to every one who gives Rome all he has.' Matthew of Paris is equally uncomplimentary. We have spoken already of the licentious young Étienne de Garlande and his proposal of going to Rome to buy the curia's consent to his installation in a bishopric ; also of the rumour that Pope Paschal disapproved, out of avarice, the censure passed on the adulterous king. Duboulai, after giving Fulques's letter, is content to say that the pope feared too great an interference with the officials of the curia on account of the papal schism.

Whether the letter of the monastic diplomatist had any weight with Abélard or no, it seems that he did desist from his plan, and laid aside all thought of Fulbert. But the unfortunate monk soon discovered the disastrous error he had made in seeking peace at the abbey of St. Denis. There had, in fact, been a serious mistake on both sides. The monks welcomed one whom they only knew as a lively, witty, interesting associate, a master of renown, a poet and musician of merit. A new attraction would accrue to their abbey, a new distraction to their own life, by the admission of Abélard. The diversion of the stream of scholars from Paris to St. Denis would bring increased colour, animation, and wealth. The erudite troubadour and brilliant scholar would be an excellent companion in the refectory, when the silent meal was over, and the wine invited conversation.

They were rudely awakened to their error when Abélard began to lash them with mordant irony for their 'intolerable uncleanness.' They found that the love-inspired songster was dead. They had introduced a kind of Bernard of Clairvaux, a man of wormwood valleys, into their happy abbey: a morose, ascetic, sternly consistent monk, who poured bitter scorn on the strong wines and pretty maids, the high festivals and pleasant excursions, with which the brothers smoothed the rough path to Paradise. And when the gay Latin Quarter transferred itself to St. Denis, and clamoured for the brilliant master, Abélard utterly refused to teach. Abbot Adam gently remonstrated with his 'subject,' pointing out that he ought now to do more willingly for the honour of God and the sake of his brothers in religion what he had formerly done out of worldly and selfish interest. Whereupon Abbot Adam was urgently reminded of a few truths, nearly con-

cerning himself and 'the brothers,' which, if not
new to his conscience, were at least novel to
his ears.

So things dragged on for a while, but Adam
was forced at length to rid the monastery of
the troublesome monk.   Finding a pretext in
the importunity of the students, he sent Abélard
down the country to erect his chair in one of
the dependencies of the abbey.   These country-
houses have already been mentioned.   Large
estates were left to the abbey in various parts of
the country.   Monks had to be sent to these
occasionally, to collect the revenue from the
farmers and millers, and, partly for their own
convenience, partly so that they might return
something in spiritual service to the district, they
built 'cells' or 'oratories' on the estates.   Frequently the cell became a priory; not infrequently
it rebelled against the mother-house ; nearly
always, as is the experience of the monastic
orders at the present day, it was a source of
relaxation and decay.

The precise locality of the 'cell' which was
entrusted to Brother Peter is matter of dispute,
and the question need not delay us.   It was
somewhere on the estates of Count Theobald of

Champagne, and therefore not very far from Paris. Here Abélard consented to resume his public lectures, and 'gathered his horde of barbarians about him' once more, in the jealous phrase of Canon Roscelin.

Otto von Freising relates that Abélard had now become 'more subtle and more learned than ever.' There is no reason to doubt that he continued to advance in purely intellectual power, but it seems inevitable that he must have lost much of the brightness and charm of his earlier manner. Yet his power and his fascination were as great as ever. Maisoncelle, or whatever village it was, was soon transformed into the intellectual centre of France. It is said by some historians that three thousand students descended upon the village, like a bewildering swarm of locusts. Abélard says the concourse was so great that 'the district could find neither hospitality nor food' for the students. One need not evolve from that an army of several thousand admirers, but it seems clear that there was a second remarkable gathering of students from all parts of Christendom. There was no teacher of ability to succeed him at Paris; he was still the most eminent master in Europe. Even if he had lost a little of the sparkle of his sunny years, no other master had ever possessed it.   Indeed, it is not audacious to think that the renewal of his early success and the sweetness of life in lovely Champagne may have in time quickened again such forces and graces of his character as had not been physically eradicated.   He began to see a fresh potentiality of joy in life.

Unfortunately for Abélard, his perverse destiny had sent him down to the neighbourhood of Rheims.   It will be remembered that Anselm of Laon was urged to suppress Abélard's early theological efforts by two of his fellow-pupils, Alberic of Rheims and Lotulphe of Novare. Alberic appears to have been a man of ability, and he had been made archdeacon of the cathedral, and head of the episcopal school, at Rheims.   He had associated Lotulphe with himself in the direction of the schools, and they were teaching with great success when Abélard appeared on the near horizon.   Anselm of Laon and William of Champeaux had gone, and the two friends were eager to earn the title of their successors.   The apparent extinction of Master Abélard had largely increased their prestige, and had filled the school of Rheims.   Indeed, we

gather from the details of a 'town and gown'
fight which occurred at Rheims about this time
that the students had almost come to outnumber
the citizens.

Hence it is not surprising that Abélard's new-
found peace was soon disturbed by rumours of
the lodging of complaints against him in high
quarters. The Archbishop of Rheims, Ralph the
Green, began to be assailed with charges. In the
first place, he was reminded, it was uncanonical
for a monk to give lectures, and take up a per-
manent residence, outside his monastery; moreover, the said monk was most unmonastically
engaged in reading Aristotle, with a flavour of
Vergil, Ovid, and Lucan. Raoul le Vert probably
knew enough about St. Denis not to attempt
to force Abélard to return to it. Then the
grumblers—'chiefly those two early intriguers,'
says the victim—urged that Abélard was teaching
without a 'respondent'; but the archbishop still
found the pretext inadequate. Then, at length,
came the second great cloud, the accusation of
heresy.

The convert had now made theology his chief
object of study. The students who gathered
about him in his village priory loudly demanded

a resumption of the lectures on dialectics and rhetoric, but Abélard had really passed to a new and wholly religious outlook. He complied with the request, only with a secret intention that, as he states in the 'Story,' philosophy should be used as a bait in the interest of divinity. The religious welfare of his followers now seriously concerned him. It will be seen presently that he exercised a strict control over their morals, and it was from the purest of motives that he endeavoured, by a pious diplomacy, to direct their thoughts to the study of Holy Writ. His rivals and enemies have attempted to censure him for this casting of pearls before swine. Certainly there were dangers accompanying the practice, but these were not confined to Abélard's school. We can easily conceive the disadvantage of discussing the question, for instance, *utrum Maria senserit dolorem vel delectationem in Christo concipiendo?* before a crowd of twelfth century students. However, Abélard's attitude was wholly reverent, and his intention as pure as that of St. Anselm.

The one characteristic feature of Abélard's theological work — the feature which was constantly seized by his enemies, and which invests him with so great an interest for the modern

student—was his concern to conciliate human
reason.   His predecessors had complacently
affirmed that reason had no title to respect in
matters of faith.   They insulted it with such
pious absurdities as 'I believe in order that I
may understand' and 'Faith goeth before under-
standing.'   Abélard remained until his last hour
constitutionally incapable of adopting that attitude.
He frequently attributes his obvious concern to
meet the questioning of reason to the desire of
helping his followers.   This is partly a faithful
interpretation of their thoughts—for which, however, he himself was chiefly responsible — and
partly a subtle projection of his own frame of
mind into his hearers.   The development of the
reasoning faculty which was involved in so keen
a study of dialectics was bound to find expression
in rationalism.

Abélard seems already to have written two
works of a very remarkable character for his
age.   One of these is entitled *A Dialogue between a Philosopher, a Jew, and a Christian*.   It
may have been founded on the *Octavius* of
Minucius Felix ; on the other hand it may be
classed with Lessing's *Nathan*.   It has been called
' the most radical expression of his rationalism,'

and it would certainly seem to embody his attitude during the period of his highest prosperity. The ultimate victory lies with the Christian, so far as the work goes (it is unfinished), but incidentally it shows more than one bold departure from traditional formulæ. Abélard's reluctance to consign all the heathen philosophers to Tartarus would be highly suspect to his pious contemporaries. It is a matter of faith in the Roman Catholic Church to-day that no man shall enter heaven who has not a belief in a personal God, at least; many theologians add the narrower qualification of a literal acceptance of the Trinity. But Abélard tempered his audacity by proving that his favourite heathens *had* this qualification of a knowledge of the Trinity, probably under the inspiration of St. Augustine.

The *Dialogue* was not much assailed by his rivals; probably it was not widely circulated. It is, however, an important monument of Abélard's genius. It anticipated not merely the rationalistic attitude of modern theology, but also quite a number of the modifications of traditional belief which modern rational and ethical criticism has imposed. Abélard regards the ethical content of Christianity, and finds that it is only the elaboration or the reformation of the natural law, the true essence of religion. God has given this essential gift in every conscience and in every religion ; there are no outcasts from the plan of salvation ; the higher excellence of the Christian religion lies in its clearer formulation of the law of life. The popular notions of heaven and hell and deity are travesties of true Christian teaching. God, as a purely spiritual being, is the supreme good, and heaven is an approach to Him by obedience ; hell, isolation from Him. When we remember that Abélard had before him only the works of the fathers and such recent speculations as those of Anselm, we shall surely recognise the action of a mind of the highest order in these debates.

The second work was not less remarkable. It was a collection of sentences from the fathers on points of dogma. So far the compilation would be an admirable one, but apart from the growing accusation that Abélard was wanting in reverence for the authority of the fathers, there was the suspicious circumstance that he had grouped these eighteen hundred texts in contradictory columns. Thus one hundred and fifty-eight questions are put by the compiler, relating

to God, the Trinity, the Redemption, the Sacra-
ments, and so forth.   The quotations from the
fathers are then arranged in two parallel
columns, one half giving an affirmative, and the
rest a negative, answer to the question.   Such
a work would be perfectly intelligible if it came
from the pen of a modern freethinker.   Abélard's
Sic et Non (Yes and No), as the work came
to be called, has borne many interpretations.
Such careful and impartial students of Abélard's
work as Deutsch pronounce the critical element
in it to be 'constructive, not sceptical.'   Most
probably it was the intention of the compiler to
shatter the excessive regard of his contemporaries
for the words of the fathers, and thus to open
the way for independent speculation on the deposit of revelation (to which he thought he had
as much right as Jerome or Augustine), by making
a striking exhibition of their fallibility.

Neither of these works seems to have fallen
into the hands of Alberic.   Twenty years afterwards we find a theologian complaining of the
difficulty of obtaining some of Abélard's works,
which had been kept secret.   He probably refers
to one or both of these works.   However that
may be, Abélard wrote a third book during his

stay at Maisoncelle, and on this the charge of heresy was fixed.

Wiser than the Church of those days, and anticipating the wisdom of the modern Church of Rome, Abélard saw the great danger to the faith itself of the Anselmian maxim, *Fides praecedit intellectum.* He argued that, as the world had somehow outlived the age of miracles, God must have intended rational evidence to take its place. In any case, there was an increasingly large class of youths and men who clamoured for 'human and philosophic grounds,' as he puts it, who would lie to their consciences if they submitted to the current pietism. Abélard believed he would render valuable service to the Church if he could devise rational proofs, or at least analogies, of its dogmas. It was in this frame of mind, not in a spirit of destructive scepticism, that he raised the standard of rationalism. He at once applied his force to the most preterrational of dogmas, and wrote his famous *Treatise on the Unity and Trinity of God.*

A manuscript of the treatise was discovered by Stölzle a few years ago. It is unnecessary to inflict on the reader an analysis of the work. It is perfectly sincere and religious in intention, but, like every book that has ever been penned on the subject of the Trinity, it contains illustrations which can be proved to be heretical. We may discuss the point further apropos of the Council of Soissons.

CHAPTER VII

THE TRIAL OF A HERETIC

THE swiftly multiplying charges seem to have impaired Abélard's health.   He became much more sensitive to the accusation of heresy than the mere injustice of it can explain.   We have an evidence of his morbid state at this period in a letter he wrote to the Bishop of Paris.   The letter must not be regarded as a normal indication of the writer's character, but, like the letter of Canon Roscelin which it elicited, it is not a little instructive about the age in which the writers lived. There are hypercritical writers who question the correctness of attributing these letters to Abélard and Roscelin, but the details they contain refer so clearly to the two masters that any doubt about their origin is, as Deutsch says, 'frivolous and of no account'; he adds that we should be only too glad, for the sake of the writers, if there were

some firm ground for contesting their genuine-
ness.

A pupil of Abélard's, coming down from Paris,
brought him word that Roscelin had lodged an
accusation of heresy against him with the bishop.
As a monk of St. Denis, Abélard still belonged
to Bishop Girbert's jurisdiction.   Roscelin had
himself been condemned for heresy on the Trinity
at Soissons in 1092, but his was an accommodating
rationalism ; he was now an important member
of the chapter of St. Martin at Tours.   Report
stated that he had discovered heresy in Abélard's
new work, and was awaiting the return of Girbert
to Paris in order to submit it to him.   Abélard
immediately grasped the pen, and forwarded to
Girbert a letter which is a sad exhibition of
' nerves.'   ' I have heard,' he says, after an ornate
salutation of the bishop and his clergy, ' that that
ever inflated and long-standing enemy of the
Catholic faith, whose manner of life and teaching
are notorious, and whose detestable heresy was
proved by the fathers of the Council of Soissons,
and punished with exile, has vomited forth many
calumnies and threats against me, on account of
the work I have written, which was chiefly directed
against his heresy.'   And so the violent and exag-

gerated account of Roscelin's misdeeds continues.
The practical point of the epistle is that Abélard
requests the bishop to appoint a place and time
for him to meet Roscelin face to face and defend
his work. The whole letter is marred by nervous
passion of the most pitiful kind. It terminates
with a ridiculous, but characteristic, dialectical
thrust at the nominalist : 'in that passage of
Scripture where the Lord is said to have eaten
a bit of broiled fish, he [Roscelin] is compelled
to say that Christ ate, not a part of the reality,
but a part of the term " broiled fish."'

Roscelin replied directly to Abélard, besides
writing to Girbert. The letter is no less characteristic of the time, though probably an equally
unsafe indication of the character of the writer.
' If,' it begins, in the gentle manner of the time,
' you had tasted a little of that sweetness of the
Christian religion which you profess by your
habit, you would not, unmindful of your order
and your profession, and forgetful of the countless
benefits you received from my teaching from your
childhood to youth, have so far indulged in words
of malice against me as to disturb the brethren's
peace with the sword of the tongue, and to
contemn our Saviour's most salutary and easy

commands.' He accepts, with an equally edifying
humility, Abélard's fierce denunciation : 'I see
myself in your words as in a mirror. Yet God
is powerful to raise up out of the very stones,'
etc. But he cannot long sustain the unnatural
tone, and he suddenly collapses into depths of
mediæval Latin, which for filth and indecency
rival the lowest productions of Billingsgate. The
venerable canon returns again and again, in the
course of his long letter, to Abélard's mutilation,
and with the art of a Terence or a Plautus. As
to the proposed debate, he is only too eager for
it. If Abélard attempts to shirk it at the last
moment, he 'will follow him all over the world.'
He finally dies away in an outburst of childish
rage which beats Abélard's peroration. He will
not continue any longer because it occurs to him
that Abélard is, by the strictest force of logic, a
nonentity. He is not a monk, for he is giving
lessons ; he is not a cleric, for he has parted with
the soutane ; he is not a layman, for he has the
tonsure ; he is not even the Peter he signs himself,
for Peter is a masculine name.

These were the two ablest thinkers of Christendom at the time. Fortunately for both, the battle
royal of the dialecticians did not take place.

Possibly Roscelin had not lodged the rumoured complaint at all. In any case Girbert was spared a painful and pitiful scene.

A short time afterwards, however, Alberic and Lotulphe found an excellent opportunity to take action. Some time in the year 1121 a papal legate, Conon, Bishop of Præneste, came to Rheims. Conon had been travelling in France for some years as papal legate, and since it was the policy of Rome to conciliate France, in view of the hostility of Germany, the legate had a general mission to make himself as useful and obliging as possible. Archbishop Ralph, for his part, would find it a convenient means of gratifying his teachers, without incurring much personal responsibility. The outcome of their conferences was, therefore, that Abélard received from the legate a polite invitation to appear at a provincial synod, or council, which was to be held at Soissons, and to bring with him his 'celebrated work on the Trinity.' The simple monk was delighted at the apparent opportunity of vindicating his orthodoxy. It was his first trial for heresy.

When the time drew near for what Abélard afterwards called 'their conventicle,' he set out for Soissons with a small band of friends, who

were to witness the chastisement of Alberic and
Lotulphe. But those astute masters had not so
naïve a view of the function of a council. Like
St. Bernard, with whom, indeed, they were already
in correspondence, they relied largely on that art
of ecclesiastical diplomacy which is the only visible
embodiment of the Church's supernatural power.
Moreover, they had the curious ecclesiastical habit
of deciding that an end—in this case, the condemnation of Abélard—was desirable, and then
piously disregarding the moral quality of the
means necessary to attain it. How far the two
masters had arranged all the conditions of the
council we cannot say, but these certainly favoured
their plans.

Soissons, to begin with, was excellently suited
for the holding of a council which was to condemn, rather than investigate. Its inhabitants
would remember the sentence passed on Roscelin
for a like offence. In fact Longueval says, in
his *Histoire de l'Église Gallicane*, that the people
of Soissons were religious fanatics as a body, and
had of their own impulse burned, or 'lynched,'
a man who was suspected of Manichæism, only
a few years previously. Alberic and Lotulphe
had taken care to revive this pious instinct, by

spreading amongst the people the information
that 'the foreign monk,' 'the eunuch of St.
Denis,' who was coming to the town to be tried,
had openly taught the error of tri-theism. The
consequence was that when the Benedictine monk
appeared in the streets with his few admirers, he
had a narrow escape of being stoned to death by
the excited citizens. It was a rude shock to his
dream of a great dialectical triumph.

On one point, however, Abélard's simple
honesty hit upon a correct measure. He went
straight to Bishop Conon with his work, and
submitted it for the legate's perusal and personal
judgment. The politician was embarrassed. He
knew nothing whatever about theology, and would
lose his way immediately in Abélard's subtle
analogies. However, he bade Abélard take the
book to the archbishop and the two masters.
They in turn fumbled it in silence, Abélard says,
and at length told him that judgment would be
passed on it at the end of the council.

Meantime Abélard had succeeded in correcting,
to some extent, the inspired prejudice of the
townsfolk. Every day he spoke and disputed
in the streets and churches, before the council
sat, and he tells us that he seemed to make an

impression on his hearers.   Alberic, in fact, came one day with a number of his pupils for the purpose of modifying his rival's success ; though he hurriedly retreated when it was shown that his specially prepared difficulty had no force. Premising 'a few polite phrases,' he pointed out that Abélard had denied that God generated himself in the Trinity; for this statement, he carefully explained, he did not ask reasons, but an authority.   Abélard promptly turned over the page, and pointed to a quotation from St. Augustine.   It was a swift and complete victory. But Abélard must needs improve on it by accusing his accuser of heresy, and Alberic departed 'like one demented with rage.'   Priests and people were now openly asking whether the council had discovered the error to lie with itself rather than with Abélard.   They came to the last day of the council.

Before the formal opening of the last session, the legate invited the chief actors in the comedy (except Abélard) to a private discussion of the situation.   Conon's position and attitude were purely political.   He cared little about their dialectical subtleties ; was, in fact, quite incompetent to decide questions of personality, modality,

and all the rest. Still it was mainly a minor
political situation he had to deal with, and he
shows an eagerness to get through it with as little
moral damage as possible. Ralph the Green,
president of the council, knew no more than
Conon about theology ; he also regarded it as
a political dilemma, and the prestige of his school
would gain by the extinction of Abélard. Ralph
had nine suffragan bishops, but only one of these
is proved to have taken part in the 'conventicle.'
It was Lisiard de Crespy, Bishop of Soissons, who
would support his metropolitan. Joscelin, an
earlier rival of Abélard, was teaching in Soissons
at that time, and would most probably accompany
his bishop. Abbot Adam of St. Denis was
present ; so were Alberic and Lotulphe. One
man of a more worthy type sat with them, an
awkward and embarrassing spokesman of truth
and justice, Geoffroi, Bishop of Chartres, one of
the most influential and most honourable members
of the French episcopacy.

Conon at once shrewdly introduced the formal
question, what heresy had been discovered in
Abélard's book ? After his ill-success in the
street-discussion, Alberic seems to have hesitated
to quote any definite passage in the work.

Indeed, we not only have two contradictory charges given, but the texts which seem to have been used in this council to prove the charge of tri-theism were quoted by the Council of Sens in 1141 in proof of an accusation of Sabellianism. Otto von Freising says that Abélard held the three divine persons to be modifications of one essence (the Anselmists claiming that the three were *realities*) ; Abélard himself says he was accused of tri-theism.   Every 'analogy' that has been found in the natural world for the dogma of the Trinity, from the shamrock of St. Patrick to the triangle of Père Lacordaire, exposes its discoverer to one or other of those charges— for an obvious reason.   After the death of Dr. Dale I remember seeing a passage quoted by one of his panegyrists in illustration of his singularly sound and clear presentation of dogma : it was much more Sabellian than anything Abélard ever wrote.

However, the explicit demand of the legate for a specimen of Abélard's heresy was embarrassing.   Nothing could be discovered in the book to which Abélard could not have assigned a parallel in the fathers.   And when Alberic began to extort heresy by ingenious interpretation Geoffroi de Lèves reminded them of the elementary rules of justice. In the formal proceedings of a trial for heresy no one was condemned unheard. If they were to anticipate the trial by an informal decision, the requirement of justice was equally urgent. They must give the accused an opportunity of defending himself. That was the one course which Alberic dreaded most of all, and he so well urged the magical power of Abélard's tongue that the bishop's proposal was rejected. Geoffroi then complained of the smallness of the council, and the injustice of leaving so grave and delicate a decision to a few prelates. Let Abélard be given into the care of his abbot, who should take him back to St. Denis and have him judged by an assembly of expert theologians. The legate liked the idea. The Rheims people regarded it, for the moment, as an effective removal of Abélard from their neighbourhood. The proposal was agreed to, and the legate then proceeded to say the Mass of the Holy Ghost.

Meantime Archbishop Ralph informed Abélard of the decision. Unsatisfactory as the delay was, he must have been grateful for an escape from the power of Rheims. He turned indifferently from the further session of the council. Unfortunately another conference was even then taking place between Alberic, Ralph, and Conon; and Abélard was presently summoned to bring his book before the council.

Alberic and Lotulphe were, on reflection, dissatisfied with the result. Their influence would have no weight in a trial at Paris, and their ambition required the sacrifice of the famous master. They therefore went to the archbishop with a complaint that people would take it to be a confession of incompetency if he allowed the case to go before another court. The three approached the legate again, and now reminded him that Abélard's work was published without episcopal permission, and could justly be condemned on that ground. As ignorant of canon law as he was of theology, and seeing the apparent friendlessness of Abélard, and therefore the security of a condemnation, Conon agreed to their proposal.

Abélard had long looked forward to the hour of his appearance before the Council. It was to be an hour of supreme triumph. The papal legate and the archbishop in their resplendent robes in the sanctuary; the circle of bishops and abbots and canons; the crowd of priests, theologians,

masters, and clerics; the solemn pulpit of the
cathedral church, from which he should make his
highest effort of dialectics and oratory; the scattered rivals, and the triumphant return to his
pupils. He had rehearsed it daily for a month or
more. But the sad, heart-rending reality of his
appearance! He was brought in, condemned.
He stood in the midst of the thronged cathedral,
with the brand of heresy on his brow, he, the intellectual and moral master of them all. A fire
was kindled there before the Council. There was
no need for Geoffrey of Chartres to come, the
tears coursing down his cheeks, to tell him his
book was judged and condemned. Quietly, but
with a fierce accusation of God Himself in his
broken heart, as he afterwards said, he cast his
treasured work in the flames.

Even in that awful moment the spirit of comedy
must needs assert its mocking presence; or is it
only part of the tragedy? Whilst the yellow
parchment crackled in the flames, some one who
stood by the legate muttered that one passage in
it said that God the Father alone was omnipotent.
Soulless politician as he was, the ignorant legate
fastened on the charge as a confirmation of the
justice of his sentence. 'I could scarcely believe

that even a child would fall into such an error,' said the brute, with an affectation of academic dignity.' 'And yet,' a sarcastic voice fell on his ear, quoting the Athanasian Creed, 'and yet there are not Three omnipotent, but One.' The bold speaker was Tirric, the Breton scholastic, who, as we have seen, probably instructed Abélard in mathematics. His bishop immediately began to censure him for his neat exhibition of the legate's ignorance, but the teacher was determined to express his disgust at the proceedings. 'You have condemned a child of Israel,' he cried, lashing the 'conventicle' with the scornful words of Daniel, 'without inquiry or certainty. Return ye to the judgment seat, and judge the judges.'

The archbishop then stepped forward to put an end to the confusion. 'It is well,' he said, making a tardy concession to conscience, 'that the brother have an opportunity of defending his faith before us all.' Abélard gladly prepared to do so, but Alberic and Lotulphe once more opposed the idea. No further discussion was needed, they urged. The council had finished its work; Abélard's errors had been detected and corrected. If it were advisable to have a profession of faith from Brother Peter, let him recite the Athanasian Creed. And lest Abélard should object that he did not know the Creed by heart, they produced a copy of it. The politic prelates were easily induced to take their view. In point of fact the archbishop's proposal was a bare compliance with the canons. Abélard's book had been condemned on the ground that it had been issued without authorisation; nothing had been determined as to the legitimacy of its contents. The canons still demanded that he should be heard before he was sent out into the world with an insidious stigma of heresy.

But charity and justice had no part in that pitiful conventicle. Archbishop and legate thought it politic to follow the ruling of Alberic to the end, and the parchment was handed to Abélard. And priest and prelate, monk and abbot, shamelessly stood around, whilst the greatest genius of the age, devoted to religion in every gift of his soul, as each one knew, faltered out the familiar symbol. ' Good Jesus, where wert thou ? ' Abélard asks, long years afterwards. There are many who ask it to-day.

So ended the holy Council of Soissons, Provincial Synod of the arch-diocese of Rheims, held under the ægis of a papal legate, in the year of grace

1121.   Its *acta* are not found in Richard, or Labbé, or Hefele : they ' have not been preserved.' There is an earlier ecclesiastical council that earned the title of the *latrocinium* (' rogues' council '), and we must not plagiarise. Ingenious and audacious as the apologetic historian is, he has not attempted to defend the Council of Soissons. But his condemnation of it is mildness itself compared with his condemnation of Abélard.

For a crowning humiliation Abélard was consigned by the council to a large monastery near Soissons, which served as jail or penitentiary for that ecclesiastical province. The abbot of this monastery, Geoffrey of the Stag's-neck, had assisted at the council, and Dom Gervaise would have it that he had secured Abélard for his own purposes. He thinks the abbot was looking to the great legal advantage, in the frequent event of a lawsuit, of having such an orator as Abélard in his monastery. It is a possibility, like many other details in Gervaise's *Life of Abélard*. In forbidding his return either to Maisoncelle or to St. Denis, and definitely consigning him to the abbey of St. Médard, the council was once more treating him as a legally convicted heretic. As far as it was concerned, it was filling the chalice of the poor monk's bitterness. It is a mere accident that Geoffrey was a man of some culture, and was so far influenced by the hideous spectacle he had witnessed as to receive Brother Peter with sympathy and some honour.

CHAPTER VIII

CLOUD UPON CLOUD

The abbey of St. Médard, to which Abélard accompanied his friendly jailer, was a very large monastery on the right bank of the Aisne, just outside Soissons. At that time it had a community of about four hundred monks. It derived a considerable revenue from its two hundred and twenty farms, yet it bore so high a repute for regular discipline that it had become a general 'reformatory school' for the district. 'To it were sent the ignorant to be instructed, the depraved to be corrected, the obstinate to be tamed,' says a work of the time ; though it is not clear how Herr Hausrath infers from this that the abbey also served the purpose of monastic asylum. For this character of penitentiary the place was chosen for the confinement of Abélard. Thither he retired to meditate on the joy and the wisdom of 'conversion.' 'God ! How furiously did I accuse Thee!' he says of those days. The earlier wound had been preceded, he admits, by his sin; this far deeper and more painful wound had been brought upon him by his 'love of our faith.'

Whether Abbot Geoffrey thought Abélard an acquisition or no, there was one man in authority at St. Médard who rejoiced with a holy joy at his advent. This was no other than Abélard's earlier acquaintance, St. Goswin. The zealous student had become a monastic reformer, and had recently been appointed Prior[1] of St. Médard. In the recently reformed abbey, with a daily arrival of 'obstinate monks to be trained,' and a convenient and well-appointed ascetical armoury or whipping-room, the young saint was in a congenial element. Great was his interest when 'Pope Innocent,'[2] as his biographers say, 'sent Abélard to be confined in the abbey, and, like an untamed rhinoceros, to be caught in the bonds of discipline.' Abélard was not long in the abbey before the tamer approached this special task that Providence had set him. We can imagine Abélard's feelings

[1] A prior is the second in command in an abbey, or the head of a priory; a priory was a small branch monastery, in those days, though it may now, as with the Dominicans, be a chief house.

[2] This is erroneous; Calixtus II. filled the papal chair at the time.

when the obtuse monk took him aside, and ex-
horted him 'not to think it a misfortune or an
injury that he had been sent there ; he was not
so much confined in a prison, as protected from
the storms of the world.' He had only to live
piously, and set a good example, and all would
be well. Abélard was in no mood to see the
humour of the situation. He peevishly retorted
that 'there were a good many who talked about
piety and did not know what piety was.' Then
the prior, say his biographers, saw that it was not
a case for leniency, but for drastic measures.
'Quite true,' he replied, 'there are many who
talk about piety, and do not know what it is.
But if we find you saying or doing anything that
is not pious, we shall show you that we know
how to treat its contrary, at all events.' The
saint prevailed once more—in the biography :
'the rhinoceros was cowed, and became very
quiet, more patient under discipline, more fearful
of the lash, and of a saner and less raving
mind.'

Fortunately, the boorish saint had a cultured
abbot, one at least who did not hold genius to
be a diabolical gift, and whose judgment of
character was not wholly vitiated by the crude

mystic and monastic ideal of the good people of the period. The abbot seems to have saved Abélard from the zeal of the prior, and possibly he found companionable souls amongst the four hundred monks of the great abbey, some of whom were nobles by birth. We know, at all events, that in the later period he looked back on the few months spent at St. Médard with a kindly feeling.

His imprisonment did not last long. When the proceedings of the council were made known throughout the kingdom, there was a strong outburst of indignation. It must not be supposed that the Council of Soissons illustrates or embodies the spirit of the period or the spirit of the Church ; this feature we shall more nearly find in the Council of Sens, in 1141. The conventicle had, in truth, revealed some of the evils of the time : the danger of the Church's excessively political attitude and administration, the brutality of the spirit it engendered with regard to heresy, the fatal predominance of dogma over ethic. But, in the main, the conventicle exhibits the hideous triumph of a few perverse individuals, who availed themselves of all that was crude and ill-advised in the machinery of the Church.

When, therefore, such men as Tirric, and Geoffrey of Chartres, and Geoffrey of the Stag's-neck, spread their story abroad, there were few who did not sympathise with Abélard. The persecutors soon found it necessary to defend themselves; there was a chaos of mutual incriminations. Even Alberic and Lotulphe tried to cast the blame on others. The legate found it expedient to attribute the whole proceeding openly to 'French malice.' He had been 'compelled for a time to humour their spleen,' as Abélard puts it, but he presently revoked the order of confinement in St. Médard, and gave Abélard permission to return to St. Denis.

It was a question of Scylla or Charybdis, of Prior Goswin or Abbot Adam. The legate seems to have acted in good faith in granting the permission—perhaps we should say in good policy, for he again acted out of discreet regard for circumstances; but when we find Abélard availing himself of what was no more than a permission to return to St. Denis we have a sufficient indication of the quality of his experience at St. Médard. He does indeed remark that the monks of the reformed abbey had been friendly towards him, though this is inspired by an obvious comparison with his later experience at St. Denis. But St. Médard was a prison ; that sufficed to turn the scale. A removal from the penitentiary would be equivalent, in the eyes of France, to a revocation of the censure passed on him. So with a heart that was hopelessly drear, not knowing whether to smile or weep, he went back, poor sport of the gods as he was, to the royal abbey.

For a few months Brother Peter struggled bravely with the hard task the fates had set him. He was probably wise enough to refrain from inveighing, in season and out of season, against the 'intolerable uncleanness' of Adam and his monks. Possibly he nursed a hope—or was nursed by a hope—of having another 'cell' entrusted to his charge. In spite of the irregularity of the abbey, formal religious exercises were extensively practised. All day and night the chant of the breviary was heard in the monastic chapel. There was also a large and busy *scriptorium* ; the *archivium* of the ancient abbey was a treasury of interesting old documents ; and there was a relatively good library. It was in the latter that Brother Peter found his next adventure, and one that threatened to be the most serious of all.

Seeing the present futility of his theological plans, he had turned to the study of history. There was a copy of Bede's *History of the Apostles* in the library, and he says that he one day, 'by chance,' came upon the passage in which Bede deals with St. Denis. The Anglo-Saxon historian would not admit the French tradition about St. Denis. He granted the existence of a St. Denis, but said that he had been Bishop of Corinth, not of Athens. The legend about the martyrdom of Denis the Areopagite, with his companions Rusticus and Eleutherius, at Paris in the first century, is now almost universally rejected by Roman Catholic historians, not to mention others. It is, however, still enshrined with honour in that interesting compendium of myths of the Christian era, the Roman breviary, and is read with religious solemnity by every priest and every monastic choir in the Catholic world on the annual festival.

However, the abbey of St. Denis, the monastery that owed all its wealth and repute to its possession of the bones of 'the Areopagite,' was the last place in the world in which to commence a rationalistic attack on the legend. With his usual want of tact and foresight Brother Peter showed the passage in Bede to some of his fellow-monks, 'in joke,' he says ; he might as well have cut the abbot's throat, or destroyed the wine-cellar 'in joke.' There was a violent commotion. Heresy about the Trinity was bad, but heresy about the idol of the royal abbey was more touching. It is not quite clear that Abélard came to the opinion of modern religious historians, that the St. Denis of Paris was a much later personage than the Areopagite of the Acts of the Apostles, but he seems to hold that opinion. In any case, the monks felt that to be the substance of his discovery, and held it to be an attack on the glory of the abbey. Venerable Bede was, they bluntly replied, a liar. One of their former abbots, Hilduin, had made a journey to Greece for the special purpose of verifying the story.

When the monks flew to Abbot Adam with the story of Brother Peter's latest outbreak, Adam saw in it an opportunity of terrifying the rebel into submission, if not of effectually silencing him. He called a chapter of the brethren. One's pen almost tires of describing the cruel scenes to which those harsh days lent themselves. The vindictive abbot perched on his high chair, prior and elder brethren sitting beside him ; the hundreds of black-robed, shaven monks lining the room ; on his knees in the centre the pale, nervous figure of the Socrates of Gaul. With a mock solemnity, Abbot Adam delivers himself of the sentence. Brother Peter has crowned his misdeeds, in his pride of mind, with an attack, not merely on the abbey that sheltered him, but on the honour and the safety of France. The matter is too serious to be punished by even the most severe methods at the command of the abbey. Brother Peter is to be handed over to the king, as a traitor to the honour of the country. The poor monk, now thoroughly alarmed, abjectly implores the abbot to deal with him in the usual way. Let him be scourged— anything to escape the uncertain temper of King Louis. No, the abbey must be rid of him. He is taken away into confinement, with an injunction that he be carefully watched until it is convenient to send him to Paris.

There were, however, some of the monks who were disgusted at the savage proceeding. A few days afterwards he was assisted to escape from the monastic dungeon during the night, and, ' in utter despair,' he fled from the abbey, with a few of his former pupils. It was, in truth, a desperate move. As a deserter from the abbey, the canons required that two stalwart brothers should be sent in pursuit of him, and that he be reimprisoned. As a fugitive from the king's justice, to which he had been publicly destined, he was exposed to even harsher treatment. However, he made his way into Champagne once more, and threw himself on the mercy of his friends.

One of the friends whom he had attached to himself during his stay at Maisoncelle was prior of St. Ayoul, near the gates of Provins. It was a priory belonging to the monks of Troyes, and both Hatton, Bishop of Troyes, and Theobald, Count of Champagne, were in sympathy with the fugitive. The prior, therefore, received Abélard into his convent, to afford at least time for reflection. His condition, however, was wholly uncanonical, and the prior, as well as the abbot of St. Peter of Troyes, urged him to secure some regularity for his absence from St. Denis, so that they might lawfully shelter him at St. Ayoul. Abélard summoned what diplomatic faculty he had, and wrote to St. Denis.

'Peter, monk by profession and sinner by his deeds, to his dearly beloved father, Adam, and to

his most dear brethren and fellow-monks,' was
the inscription of the epistle. Brother Peter, it
must be remembered, was fighting almost for
life; and he was not of the heroic stuff of his
friend and pupil, Arnold of Brescia. There are
critics who think he descended lower than this
concession to might, that he deliberately denied
his conviction for the purpose of conciliating
Adam. Others, such as Poole, Deutsch, and
Hausrath, think the letter does not support so
grave a censure. The point of the letter is
certainly to convey the impression that Bede had
erred, and that Abélard had no wish to urge his
authority against the belief of the monks. In
point of fact, Bede is at variance with Eusebius
and Jerome, and it is not impossible that Abélard
came sincerely to modify the first impression he
had received from Bede's words; in the circumstances, and in the then state of the question,
this would not be unreasonable. At the same
time a careful perusal of the letter gives one the
impression that it is artistic and diplomatic; that
Abélard has learned tact, rather than unlearned
history. It reads like an effort to say something
conciliatory about St. Denis, without doing serious
violence to the writer's conscience. Perhaps the

abbot of St. Peter's could have thrown some light on its composition.

Shortly afterwards Abbot Adam came to visit Count Theobald, and Abélard's friends made a direct effort to conciliate him. The prior of St. Ayoul and Abélard hurried to the count's castle, and begged him to prevail upon his guest to release Abélard from his obedience. The count tried to persuade Adam to do so, but without success. Adam seemed determined, not so much to rid his happy convent of a malcontent, as to crush Abélard. He found plenty of pious garbs to cover his vindictiveness with. At first he deprecated the idea that it was a matter for his personal decision. Then, after a consultation with the monks who accompanied him, he gravely declared that it was inconsistent with the honour of the abbey to release Abélard; 'the brethren had said that, whereas Abélard's choice of their abbey had greatly redounded to its glory, his flight from it had covered them with shame.' He threatened both Abélard and the prior of St. Ayoul with the usual canonical penalties, unless the deserter returned forthwith to obedience.

Adam's departure, after this fulmination, left

Abélard and his friends sadly perplexed. The abbot had the full force of canon law on his side, and he was evidently determined to exact his pound of flesh. However, whilst they were busy framing desperate resolves, they received information of the sudden death of Abbot Adam. He died a few days after leaving Champagne, on the 19th of February 1122. The event brought relief from the immediate pressure. Some time would elapse before it would be necessary to resume the matter with Adam's successor, and there was room for hope that the new abbot would not feel the same personal vindictiveness.

The monk who was chosen by the Benedictines of St. Denis to succeed Adam was one of the most remarkable characters of that curious age. Scholar, soldier, and politician, he had an enormous influence on the life of France during the early decades of the twelfth century. Nature intended him for a minister and a great soldier : chance made him a monk ; worldly brothers made him an abbot, and St. Bernard completed the anomaly by 'converting' him in 1127. At the time we are speaking of he was the more active and prominent of two men whom Bernard called 'the two calamities of the Church of France.'

He was born of poor parents, near one of the priories or dependencies of St. Denis. His talent was noticed by the monks, and his 'vocation' followed as a matter of course. He was studying in the monastic school when King Philip brought his son Louis to St. Denis, and the abbot sent for him, and made him companion to the royal pupil. He thus obtained a strong influence over the less gifted prince, and when Louis came to the throne in 1108, Suger became the first royal councillor. Being only a deacon in orders, there was nothing to prevent him heading the troops, directing a campaign, or giving his whole time to the affairs of the kingdom. He had proved so useful a minister that, when some of the monks of St. Denis came in great trepidation to tell the king they had chosen him for abbot, they were angrily thrust into prison. Suger himself was in Rome at the time, discharging a mission from the king, and he tells us, in his autobiography, of the perplexity the dilemma caused him. However, before he reached France, the king had concluded that an abbot could be as useful as a prior in an accommodating age. In the sequel, St. Denis became more royal, and less abbatial than ever— until 1127. St. Bernard complained that it seemed to have become the 'war office' and the 'ministry of justice' of the kingdom.

Abélard now seems to have been taken in hand by a more astute admirer, Burchard, Bishop of Meaux. They went to Paris together, and apparently did a little successful diplomacy before the arrival and consecration of Suger. The newly created abbot (he had been ordained priest the day before his consecration) refused to undo the sentence of his predecessor. He was bound by the decision of the abbey, he said ; in other words, there was still a strong vindictive feeling against Abélard in the abbey, which it was not politic to ignore. It is quite impossible that Suger himself took the matter seriously.

But before Suger's arrival Abélard and his companions had made friends at court. Whether through his pupils, many of whom were nobles, or through his family, is unknown, but Abélard for the second time found influence at court when ecclesiastical favour was denied. One of the leading councillors was Étienne de Garlande, the royal seneschal, and means were found to interest him in the case of the unfortunate monk. We have already seen that Stephen had ecclesiastical ambition in his earlier years, and had

M

become a deacon and a canon of Étampes. But when his patron, King Philip, submitted to the Church and to a better ideal of life, Stephen concluded that the path to ecclesiastical dignities would be less smooth and easy for the 'illiterate and unchaste,' and he turned to secular ambition. At the time of the events we are reviewing he and Suger were the virtual rulers of France; from the ecclesiastical point of view he was the man whom St. Bernard associated with Suger as 'a calamity of the Church.'

'Through the mediation of certain friends' Abélard had enlisted the interest of this powerful personage, and the court was soon known to favour his suit. There are many speculations as to the motive of the king and his councillors in intervening in the monastic quarrel. Recent German historians see in the incident an illustration of a profound policy on the part of the royal council. They think the king was then endeavouring to strengthen his authority by patronising the common people in opposition to the tyrannical and troublesome nobility. Following out a parallel policy with regard to the Church, whose nobles were equally tyrannical and troublesome, Stephen and Suger would naturally befriend the lower clergy in opposition to the prelates.   Hence the royal intervention on behalf of the monk of St. Denis is associated with the intervention on the side of the peasantry a few years before.

The theory is ingenious, but hardly necessary. Abélard says that the court interfered because it did not desire any change in the free life of the royal abbey, and consequently preferred to keep him out of it.   That is also ingenious, and complimentary to Abélard.   But it is not a little doubtful whether anybody credited him with the smallest influence at St. Denis.   We shall probably not be far from the truth if we suppose a court intrigue on the monk's behalf which his friends did not think it necessary to communicate fully to him.   Geoffrey of Chartres and other friends of his were French nobles. Many of his pupils had that golden key which would at any time give access to Étienne de Garlande.

In any case Stephen and Suger had a private discussion of the matter, and the two politicians soon found a way out of the difficulty.   Abélard received an order to appear before the king and his council.   The comedy — though it was no

comedy for Abélard — probably took place at
St. Denis. Louis the Fat presided, in robes of
solemn purple, with ermine border. Étienne de
Garlande and the other councillors glittered at
his side. Abbot Suger and his council were
there to defend the 'honour' of the abbey ; and
Brother Peter, worn with anxiety and suffering,
came to make a plea for liberty. Louis bids the
abbot declare what solution of the difficulty his
chapter has discovered. Suger gravely explains
that the honour of their abbey does not permit
them to allow the fugitive monk to join any
other monastery. So much to save the face of
the abbey. Yet there is a middle course possible,
the abbot graciously continues : Brother Peter
may be permitted to live a regular life in the
character of a hermit. Brother Peter expresses
his satisfaction at the decision — it was precisely
the arrangement he desired—and departs from
the abbey with his friends, a free man once more,
never again, he thinks, to fall into the power of
monk or prelate.

CHAPTER IX

BACK TO CHAMPAGNE

THE scene of the next act in Abélard's dramatic career is a bright, restful valley in the heart of Champagne.   It is the summer of 1122, and the limpid Arduzon rolls through enchantingly in its course towards the Seine.   In the meadow beside it are two huts and a small oratory, rudely fashioned from the branches of trees and reeds from the river, and daubed over with mud. No other sign of human presence can be seen. Abélard and one companion are the only human beings to be found for miles.   And even all thought of the cities of men and the sordid passions they shelter is arrested by the great forests of oak and beech which hem in the narrow horizon and guard the restfulness of the valley.

By the terms of Suger's decision Abélard could neither lodge with secular friends nor enter any cell, priory, or abbey.   Probably this coercion into leading an eremitical life was unnecessary. The experience of the last three years had made a hermitage of his heart; nothing would be more welcome to him than this quiet valley. It was a spot he had noticed in earlier years. In his ancient chronicle Robert of Auxerre says that Abélard had lived there before; Mr. Poole thinks it was to the same part of Champagne that he resorted on the three occasions of his going to the province of Count Theobald. That would at least have to be understood in a very loose sense. On the two former occasions he had found a home prepared, a cell and a priory, respectively; he had now to build a hut with his own hands. It was a deserted spot he had chosen, he tells us; and Heloise adds, in one of her letters, that before Abélard's coming it had been the haunt of robbers and the home of foxes and wild boars, like the neighbouring forest of Fontainebleau.

Abélard must have seen this quiet side-valley in passing along the Seine on the road to Paris. It was some twelve miles from Troyes, where he had a number of friends; and when he expressed a desire to retire to it with his companion, they obtained for him the gift of the meadow through

which the Arduzon ran. Bishop Hatton gave
them permission to build an oratory, and they
put together a kind of mud hut—'in honour of
the Blessed Trinity'!   Here the heavy heart
began once more to dream of peace. Men had
tortured him with a caricature of the divine
justice when his aim and purpose had been of
the purest. He had left their ignorant meddle-
someness and their ugly passions far away beyond
the forests.   Alone with God and with nature
in her fairest mood, he seemed to have escaped
securely from an age that could not, or would
not, understand his high ideal.

So for some time no sound was heard in the
valley but the song of the birds and the grave
talk of the two hermits and the frequent chant
in the frail temple of the Trinity. But Abélard's
evil genius was never far from him ; it almost
seems as if it only retired just frequently enough
and long enough to let his heart regain its full
power of suffering. The unpractical scholar had
overlooked a material point, the question of sustenance. Beech-nuts and beech-leaves and roots
and the water of the river become monotonous.
Abélard began to cast about for some source of
revenue. 'To dig I was not able, to beg I was

ashamed,' he says, in the familiar words. There was only one thing he could do—teach.

Probably he began by giving quiet lessons to the sons of his neighbours. He had only to let his intention be known in Troyes, and he would have as many pupils as he desired. But he soon found that, as was inevitable, he had released a torrent. The words in which he describes this third confluence of his streams of ' barbarians' do not give us the impression that he struggled against his fate. With all his genius he remained a Breton—short of memory and light of heart. The gladdening climate of mid-France and the brightness and beauty of the valley of the Seine quickened his old hopes and powers. The word ran through the kingdoms of Gaul, and across the sea and over the southern hills, that Abélard was lecturing once more. And many hundreds, probably thousands, of youths gathered their scant treasures, and turned their faces towards the distant solitude of Nogent-sur-Seine.

Then was witnessed a scene that is quite unique in the annals of education. Many centuries before, the deserts of Egypt had seen a vast crowd of men pour out from the cities, and rush eagerly into their thankless solitude. That

was under the fresh-born influence of a new
religious story, the only force thought competent
to inspire so great an abdication. The twelfth
century saw another great stream of men pouring
eagerly into a solitude where there was no luxury
but the rude beauty of nature. Week by week
the paths that led into the valley by the Arduzon
discharged their hundreds of pilgrims. The rough
justice of nature offered no advantage to wealth.
Rich and poor, noble and peasant, young and old,
they raised their mud-cabins or their moss-covered
earth-works, each with his own hand. Hundreds
of these rude dwellings dotted the meadow and
sheltered in the wood. A bundle of straw was
the only bed to be found in them. Their tables
were primitive mounds of fresh turf; the only
food a kind of coarse peasant-bread, with roots
and herbs and a draught of sweet water from the
river. The meats and wines and pretty maids
and soft beds of the cities were left far away over
the hills. For the great magician had extended
his wand once more, and the fascination of his
lectures was as irresistible as ever.

They had built a new oratory, in wood and
stone, for the loved master; and each morning,
as the full blaze of the sun fell upon the strangely

scarred face of the valley, they arose from the hay and straw, splashed or dipped in the running river, and trooped to the spot where Abélard fished for their souls with the charming bait of his philosophy. Then when the master tired of reading Scripture, and of his pathetic task of finding analogies of the infinite in the finite, they relaxed to such games and merriment as youth never leaves behind.

Discipline, however, was strict. There is a song, composed at the time by one of the pupils, which affords an instructive glimpse of the life of the strange colony. Some one seems to have informed Abélard of a group of students who were addicted to the familiar vice. He at once banished them from the colony, threatening to abandon the lectures unless they retired to Quincey. The poet of the group was an English youth, named Hilary, who had come to France a little before. Amongst his *Versus et ludi*, edited by Champollion, we find his poetic complaint of the falseness of the charge and the cruelty of their expulsion. It is a simple, vigorous, rhymed verse in Latin, with a French refrain. It is obviously intended to be sung in chorus, and it thus indirectly illustrates one of the probable recreations of the youths who were thus thrown upon their own resources.   Many another of Hilary's rough songs must have rung through the valley at night-fall.   Perhaps Abélard recovered his old gift, and contributed to the harmless gaiety of the colony. Seared and scarred as he was, there was nothing sombre or sour about his piety, save in the moments of actual persecution.   With all his keen and living faith and his sense of remorse, he remains a Breton, a child of the sunlight, sensitive to the gladdening force of the world. Not until his last year did he accept the ascetic view of pleasures which were non-ethical.   Watch-ful over the faith and morals of the colony, he would make no effort to moderate the loud song with which they responded to the warm breath of nature.

The happiness of his little world surged in the heart of the master for a time, but nature gave him a capacity for, and a taste of, manifold happiness, only that he might suffer the more. 'I had one enemy—echo,' he says in his auto-biography.   He was soon made uneasily conscious that the echo of his teaching and the echo of the glad life of the colony had reached Clairvaux.

The first definite complaint that reached his

ears referred to the dedication of his oratory.
Though formally dedicated to the Trinity, it
was especially devoted to the Holy Spirit, in the
character of Paraclete (Comforter) ; indeed both
it and the later nunnery were known familiarly
as 'the Paraclete.' Some captious critics had, it
appears, raised a question whether it was lawful
to dedicate a chapel to one isolated member of
the Trinity. The question was absurd, for the
Church frequently offers worship to the Holy
Spirit, without mentioning the Father and the
Son. The cautious Abélard, however, defends
his dedication at great length. A second attack
was made under the pretext of questioning the pro-
priety of an image of the Trinity which was found
in the oratory. Some sculptor in the colony
had endeavoured to give an ingenious repre-
sentation of the Trinity in stone. He had carved
three equal figures from one block of stone, and
had cut on them inscriptions appropriate to each
Person of the Trinity.[1] Such devices were common
in the Church, common in all Trinitarian religions,
in fact. But Abélard was credited with intentions
and interpretations in everything he did. Neither

[1] The statue was preserved in a neighbouring church until the
eighteenth century. It was destroyed at the Revolution.

of these incidents proved serious, however.   It was not until Abélard heard that Alberic and Lotulphe were inciting 'the new apostles' to assail him that he became seriously alarmed.   The new apostles were Bernard of Clairvaux and Norbert of Prémontré.

Not many leagues from the merry valley on the Arduzon was another vale that had been peopled by men from the cities.   It was a dark, depressing valley, into which the sun rarely struggled. The Valley of Wormwood men called it, for it was in the heart of a wild, sombre, chilly forest. The men who buried themselves in it were fugitives, not merely from the hot breath of the cities and the ugly deeds of their fellows, but even from the gentler inspiration of nature, even from its purest thrills.   They had had a vision of a golden city, and believed it was to be entered by the path of self-torture.   The narrow windows of their monastery let in but little of the scanty light of the valley.   With coarse bread and herbs, and a few hours' sleep on boxes of dried leaves, they made a grudging concession to the law of living.   But a joke was a sacrilege in the Valley of Wormwood, and a song a piece of supreme folly.   The only sound that told the ravens and the owls of the presence of man was the weird, minor chant for hours together, that did not even seem to break the silence of the sombre spot. By day, the white-robed, solemn shades went about their work in silence. The Great Father had made the pilgrimage to heaven so arduous a task that they dare not talk by the wayside.

Foremost among them was a frail, tense, absorbed, dominant little man. The face was white and worn with suffering, the form enfeebled with disease and exacting nervous exaltation; but there was a light of supreme strength and of joy in the penetrating eyes. He was a man who saw the golden city with so near, so living a vision, that he was wholly impatient of the trivial pleasures of earth: a man formed in the mould of world-conquerors and world-politicians, in whose mind accident had substituted a supernatural for a natural ideal: a man of such intensity and absorption of thought that he was almost incapable of admitting a doubt as to the correctness of his own judgment and purpose and the folly of all that was opposed to it: a man in whom an altruistic ethic might transform, or disguise, but could never suppress, the demand of the entire nature for self-assertion. This was

Bernard of Clairvaux, who had founded the monastery in the deepest poverty ten years before. He was soon to be the most powerful man in Christendom. And he held that, if the instinct of reasoning and the impulse of love did indeed come from God and not from the devil, they were of those whimsical gifts, such as the deity of the Middle Ages often gave, which were given with a trust they would be rejected.

The other new apostle was St. Norbert, the founder of the Premonstratensian canons. He had fruitlessly endeavoured to reform the existing order of canons, and had then withdrawn to form a kind of monastery of canons at Prémontré, not far from Laon, where he occasionally visited Anselm. His disciples entered zealously into the task of policeing the country. No disorder in faith or morals escaped their notice; and although Norbert was far behind Bernard in political ability, the man who incurred his pious wrath was in an unenviable position. He had influence with the prelates of the Church, on account of his reforms and the sanctity of his life ; he had a profound influence over the common people, not only through his stirring sermons, but also through the miracles he wrought. Abélard frequently bases his rationalistic work on the fact, which he always assumes to be uncontroverted, that the age of miracles is over. Norbert, on the contrary, let it be distinctly understood that he was a thaumaturgus of large practice. Abélard ridiculed his pretensions, and the stories told of him. Even in his later sermons we find him scornfully 'exposing' the miracles of Norbert and his companions. They used to slip medicaments unobserved into the food of the sick, he says, and accept the glory of the miracle if the fever was cured. They even attempted to raise the dead to life ; and when the corpse retained its hideous rigidity after they had lain long hours in prayer in the sanctuary, they would turn round on the simple folk in the church and upbraid them for the littleness of their faith. This poor trickery was the chief source of the power of the Premonstratensian canons over the people. Abélard could not repose and ridicule it with impunity.

These were the new apostles—'pseudo-apostles' Heloise calls them—whom Alberic and Lotulphe now incited to take up the task which they themselves dared pursue no longer. And so, says Abélard, 'they heaped shameless calumnies on me at every opportunity, and for some time brought much discredit upon me in the eyes of certain ecclesiastical as well as secular dignitaries.' We shall find that, when Abélard stands before the ecclesiastical tribunal a second time, many of his earlier friends have deserted him, and have fallen under the wide-reaching influence of St. Bernard.

But it is strenuously denied by prejudiced admirers of St. Bernard that he had anything to do with Abélard at this period. Father Hefele, for instance, thinks that Abélard is guilty of some chronological confusion in the passage quoted above; looking back on the events of his life, he has unconsciously transferred the later activity of Bernard to the earlier date, not clearly separating it in time from the work of Alberic and Norbert. Unfortunately, the 'Story of my Calamities' was written *before* Bernard commenced his open campaign against Abélard. We shall see later that this is beyond dispute. There is, then, no question of confusion.

Mr. Cotter Morison says it is 'not far short of impossible' that Bernard showed any active hostility to Abélard at that time, and he thinks the charge springs merely from an over-excited imagination. Mr. Morison is scarcely happier here than in his earlier passage. It must be understood that this reluctance to admit the correctness of Abélard's complaint is inspired by a passage in one of Bernard's letters. In writing to William of St. Thierry (ep. cccxxvii. in *Migne*), fifteen years afterwards, he excuses his inaction with regard to Abélard (whose heresies William has put before him) on the ground that he 'was ignorant of most, indeed nearly all, of these things.' This is interpreted to mean that he knew little or nothing about Abélard until 1141, and the Abélardists generally give a more or less polite intimation that it is—what Mr. Poole explicitly calls another statement of Bernard's—a lie. Cotter Morison, however, interprets 'these things' to mean 'the special details of Abélard's heresy,' and it is therefore the more strange that he should join the Bernardists in straining the historical evidence. Yet he is probably nearer to the truth than the others in his interpretation of Bernard's words. Even modern writers are too apt at times to follow the practice of the Church, in judging a statement or an action, and put it into one or other of their rigid objective categories. In such cases as this we need a very careful psychological analysis, and are prone to be misled by the Church's objective moral boxes or classifications. Most probably Bernard wrote in that convenient vagueness of mind which sometimes helps even a saint out of a difficulty, especially where the honour of the Church is involved, and which is accompanied by just a suspicion of ethical discomfort.

In reality, we may, with all sobriety, reverse Mr. Morison's statement, and say it is 'not far short of impossible' that Bernard was ignorant of, or indifferent to, Abélard's activity at that time. Ten years previously, when Bernard led his little band of white-robed monks to their wretched barn in the Vale of Bitterness, he went to Châlons to be consecrated by William of Champeaux. William conceived a very strong affection for the young abbot, and he shortly after nursed him through a long and severe illness. So great was their intimacy and so frequent their intercourse that people said Châlons and Clairvaux had changed places. This began only twelve months after William had been driven from Paris, in intense anger, by the heretical upstart, Peter Abélard. Again, Alberic was another of Bernard's intimate friends. A year or two before Abélard founded the Paraclete—that is to say, about the time of the Council of Soissons—we find Bernard 'imploring' (so even Duchesne puts it) the Pope to appoint Alberic to the vacant see of Châlons after the death of William. He failed to obtain it, but afterwards secured for him the archbishopric of Bourges. Anselm of Laon was also a friend of Bernard's. Moreover, Clairvaux was only about forty miles from Troyes, where Abélard's latest feat was the supreme topic.

It is thus quite impossible for any but a prejudiced apologist to question Bernard's interest in the life of the Paraclete and its founder. Even were he not the heresy-hunter and universal reformer that he notoriously was, we should be compelled to think that he had heard all the worst charges against Abélard over and over again before 1124. To conceive Bernard as entombed in his abbey, indifferent to everything in this world except the grave, is the reverse of the truth. Bernard had a very profound belief in what some theologians call ' the law of secondary causes '—God does not do directly what he may accomplish by means of human instruments. Prayer was necessary ; but so were vigilance, diplomacy, much running to and fro, and a vast correspondence. He watched the Church of God with the fiery zeal of a St. Paul. He knew everything and everybody: smote archbishops and kings as freely as his own monks: hunted down every heretic that appeared in France in his day: played even a large part in the politics of Rome. And we are to suppose that such a man was ignorant of the presence of the gay, rationalistic colony a few leagues away from his abbey, and of the unique character and profound importance to the Church of that vast concourse of youths; or that he refrained from examining the teaching of this man who had an unprecedented influence over the youth of France, or from using the fulness of his power against him when he found that his teaching was the reverse of all he held sacred and salutary.

We may take Abélard's statement literally. Bernard and Norbert were doing the work of his rivals, and were doing it effectively. They who had supported him at Soissons or afterwards were being poisoned against him. Count Theobald and Geoffrey of Chartres are probably two whom he had in mind. He feels that the net is being drawn close about him through the calumnies of these ubiquitous monks and canons. The peace of the valley is broken; he becomes morbidly sensitive and timorous. Whenever he hears that some synod or conventicle has been summoned he trembles with anxiety and expectation of another Soissons. The awful torture of that hour before the council comes back to him, and mingles with the thought of the power of his new enemies. He must fly from France.

Away to the south, over the Pyrenees, was a land where the poor monk would have found peace, justice, and honour. Spain was just then affording 'glory to God in heaven, and peace to men of good-will on earth' : it had been snatched from the dominion of Christianity for a century or two. So tolerant and beneficent was the reign of the Moors that even the Jews, crushed, as they were, by seven centuries of persecution, developed their finest powers under it. They were found in the front rank of every art and science ; in every field where, not cunning and astuteness, but talent of the highest order and industry, were needed to command success. The Moors had happily degenerated from the fierce proselytism of their religious prophet—whilst the Christians had proportionately enlarged on that of theirs—and their human character was asserting the high natural ideal which it always does when it breaks away from the confining bonds of a narrow dogma.

It was towards this land that Abélard turned his thoughts. It seemed useless for him to exchange one Christian land for another. A few years before, a small group of French monks had created a centre of education in a humble barn on the banks of the Cam ; but was England more tolerant than France? He remembered Roscelin's experience. There were famous schools in Italy ; but some of his most brilliant pupils at the Paraclete, such as Arnold of Brescia, had little good to say of Italy. The evil lay in Christianity itself—in that intolerance which its high claim naturally engendered.

One does not like to accept too easily this romantic proposal to find refuge under the protection of the crescent, yet Abélard's words compel us to do so. 'God knows,' he says, 'that at times I fell into so deep a despair that I proposed to go forth from Christendom and betake me to the heathens . . . to live a Christian life amid the enemies of Christ.' Possibly he would have done so, if he had had a better knowledge of Spain at that time. The Arabs of Spain were no enemies of Christ. Only a most perverse idea

of their state could make an able thinker and
teacher thus regard a life amongst them as a
matter of ultimate and desperate resort.   Had
they but conquered Europe, materially or morally,
half the problems that still harass it—or ought
to do—would have been solved long ago.   It is
pathetic to find Abélard speculating whether the
hatred of the Christians for him will not make
his path easier to the favour of the Arabs, by
producing in them an impression that he had been
unfaithful to Christian dogma.   The caliphs could
keep a watchful eye on the thoughts of professed
Mohammedan philosophers, but they cared little
about the theories of others.   Abélard, with his
pronounced tendency to concentrate on natural-
religious and ethical truths, would have found an
honoured place in Spain ; and he would quickly
have buried his dogmas there.

Abélard was spared the trial of so desperate
and dreadful a secession.   Far away on the coast
of Brittany an abbot died in 1125, and Abélard's
evil genius put it into the hearts of the monks
to offer the vacant dignity to the famous teacher.
They sent some of their number to see him at
the Paraclete.   It seemed a providential outlet
from his intolerable position.   There were abbeys

and abbeys, it was true, but his Breton optimism and trust in fate closed that avenue of speculation. Conon, Duke of Brittany, had agreed to his installation. Suger made no opposition ; he probably saw the net that was being drawn about him in France. Abélard turned sadly away from the vale of the Paraclete and the devoted colony, and faced the mists of the west and of the future. 'I came not to bring peace into the world but the sword.'

CHAPTER X

THE TRIALS OF AN ABBOT

ABÉLARD had, of course, committed another serious blunder in accepting the proffered 'dignity.' There was an error on both sides, as there had been in his first fatal assumption of the cowl ; though on this occasion the pressure behind him was greater, the alternative less clear, and the prospect at least uncertain. It will be remembered that Abélard probably studied at Locmenach in his early years. This was a branch monastery of the ancient abbey of St. Gildas at Rhuys, on the coast ; and it is not impossible that some recollection of the monks of Locmenach entered into his decision to become abbot of St. Gildas. There were probably few abbeys in France at the time which were sufficiently moral and earnest in their life to offer a congenial home to this man who is held up to the blushes of the ages as a sinner, and of whom the Church only speaks in

the low and solemn tone that befits a great scandal.
If Abélard's first and chief misfortune is that he
was a Christian, his second is that he was a monk.

The abbey of St. Gildas had reached the last
stage of monastic decay. The monks did not
accept presents of pretty maid-servants, nor receive
fine lady visitors in their abbey, like the monks of
St. Denis ; nor were they eager to have a nunnery
of sisters in religion close at hand, like the
cloistered canons. Theirs was not a case for the
application of the words of Erasmus : ' Vocantur
" patres "—et saepe sunt.' Each monk had a
respectable wife and family on the monastic estate.
The outlying farms and cottages were colonised
with the women and the little monklings ; there
was no cemetery of infant bones at or near St.
Gildas. Their monasticism consisted in the dis-
charge of their formal religious exercises in church
and choir—the chant of the Mass and of the
breviary. And when the monk had done his
day's work of seven or eight hours' chanting, he
would retire, like every other Christian, to the
bosom of his family. The half-civilised Celtic
population of the district were quite content with
this version of their duty, and did not refuse them
the customary sustenance.

Abélard's horror on discovering this state of things was equalled by the surprise of the monks when they discovered his Quixotic ideas of monastic life. They only knew Abélard as the amorous troubadour, the teacher who attracted crowds of gay and wealthy scholars wherever he went, the object of the bitter hostility of the monastic reformers whom they detested. It was the Bernardist or Norbertian Abélard whom they had chosen for their abbot. Surprise quickly turned to disgust when the new abbot lectured them in chapter—as a sexless ascetic could so well do—on the beauty of continence and the Rule of St. Benedict. They were rough, ignorant, violent men, and they soon made it clear that reform was hopelessly out of the question.

The very locality proved an affliction. He had exchanged the gentle beauty and the mild climate of the valley of the Seine for a wild, bleak, storm-swept sea-shore. The abbey was built on a small promontory that ran out into the Bay of Biscay, a few leagues to the south of Vannes. It was perched on the edge of the steep granite cliffs, and Abélard's very pen seems to shudder as he writes of the constant roar of the waves at the foot of the rocks and the sweep of the ocean winds.

Behind them stretched a long series of sand-hills.
They occupied a scarcely gracious interval between
desolation and desolation. For Abélard was not
of the temperament to appreciate the grandeur of
an ever-restless ocean or to assimilate the strength
that is borne on its winds. He was sadly troubled.
Here he had fled, he says, to the very end of the
earth, the storm-tossed ocean barring his further
retreat, yet he finds the world no less repulsive
and cruel.

In the character of abbot, Abélard was at liberty
to seek what consolation he could outside his abbey.
He soon found that there was none to be had
in the vicinity of Rhuys. 'The whole barbarous
population of the land was similarly lawless and
undisciplined,' he says; that seems to include such
other monks and priests as the locality contained.
Even their language was unintelligible to him, he
complains; for, although he was a Breton, his ear
would only be accustomed to Latin and to Romance
French, which would differ considerably from the
Celtic Bas-Breton. Whether the lord of the
district was equally wild—as seems most probable
—or no, the way to his château was barred by
another difficulty. He was considered the bitter
enemy of the abbey, for he had 'annexed' the

lands that belonged by right to the monks.
Moreover he exacted a heavy tribute from them.
They were frequently without food, and wandered
about stealing all they could lay their hands on for
the support of their wives and families. They
violently urged Abélard to fight for their rights
and find food for them, instead of giving them his
ethereal discourses. And the abbot succeeded
just far enough to embitter the usurper against
him, without obtaining much for his lawless monks.
He found himself in a new dilemma. If he
remained in the abbey he was assailed all day by
the hungry clamour and the brutal violence of his
'subjects'; if he went abroad the tyrannical lord
threatened to have him done to death by his armed
retainers.

For three or four years Abélard sustained this
miserable existence almost without alleviation. In
1129, however, an event occurred which, evil as it
looked at the moment, proved a source of considerable happiness to him for some years.

Abbot Suger, the cowled warrior and statesman,
had become monastic reformer after his conversion.
The circumstance proved more lucrative to St.
Denis than would be thought. In his *De rebus
a se gestis*, Suger writes at great length of the

additional possessions he secured for the abbey, and amongst these is enumerated the nunnery of St. Mary at Argenteuil.   He was not only a rigid disciplinarian, but he had an unusual acquaintance with ancient records.   Many of his early years at St. Denis had been spent in the *archivium*, in diligent scrutiny of deeds and documents relating to the earlier history of the abbey.   One day when he was absorbed in this study he hit upon a document from which it seemed possible to prove that the convent of the Benedictine nuns at Argenteuil, two or three miles away, belonged to the monks of St. Denis.   It was a complicated question, the nuns dating their possession from the time of Charlemagne.   But when Suger became abbot of St. Denis himself, and eager to employ his political ability and influence in the service of the abbey, he recollected, along with others, the document relating to the nunnery. When, moreover, he had been converted, he was able to see the licentiousness of the nuns of Argenteuil, and make it a pretext for asserting the rights of his abbey.

In 1127, he states in his Life, he obtained from Honorius ii. a bull which was supposed to legalise his seizure of the convent : 'both in justice to ourselves and on account of the enormity of life of the nuns who were established there, he restored the place to us with its dependencies, so that the religious life might be re-instituted in it.' In his *Vita Ludovici Grossi* he also lays stress on the 'foul enormity' of life in the nunnery.

How far we may accept the strong language of the enterprising abbot it would be difficult to say. Honorius, who would be flattered by the request to pronounce on the domestics difficulties of the Church of France, would certainly not be over-exacting in the matter of proof. Still, he sent a legate, the Bishop of Albano, and directed him to hold an inquiry into the affair, together with the Archbishop of Rheims and the Bishops of Paris, Chartres, and Soissons. The name of Geoffrey of Chartres is a guarantee that the inquiry was more than a mere cloak to cover the sanctioning of a questionable act. Although, we must remember, Suger does not quote their words in the above passage, they must have decided that his charge was substantially founded. The nuns were turned out of their convent a few months afterwards.

The asserted corruption of the nunnery is quite in accord with what we know of the period from other sources. We have already quoted Jacques de Vitry's observation that none of the convents of the time, except those of the Cistercians (his own order), were fit places for an honest woman ; and he describes the ' thousand tricks and wicked artifices' by which respectable dames were sometimes induced to enter them. The same Vandyke-like painter of the morals of the twelfth century elsewhere passes a comprehensive sentence on the convents of canonesses. Nor was this the first Parisian nunnery to be suppressed in the twelfth century. There was until 1107 a convent of Benedictine nuns on the island, on the site of the present Rue Calende. It was close to the royal palace ; and the relations of the nuns to the nobles of the court had become so notorious that Bishop Galo had to intervene and put the good sisters on the street. One has only to read Abélard's sermon on ' Susannah ' (delivered to an exemplary community of nuns) to realise the condition of the average nunnery at that time.

Heloise was prioress of the convent of Argenteuil. This is, indeed, the only circumstance that need make us hesitate to accept Suger's words at their literal value. The Heloise of those writers who have but touched the love-romance of the

o

famous couple, without entering into a deeper study
of their characters, is pitifully inadequate. She
had all the passion that poetic or decadent admirer
has ever given her ; she had that freer, because
narrower, view of the love-relation, which only
regarded her own particular and exceptional case,
and did not extend to the thousand cases on
which the broad law of matrimony is based ; and
she retained her ardent love and her particularist
view throughout long years of conventual life.
We may examine this more directly in the next
chapter. For the moment it reveals, when it is
taken in conjunction with that integrity and
altitude of life which none can hesitate to assign
her, a strength and elevation of character which
are frequently obscured by the mere admirers
of her passion. We know nothing whatever of
the eight or nine miserable years of her life at
Argenteuil ; but as soon as she does emerge into
the light of history (in 1130) she is found to be
of an elevated and commanding character. She
was prior, not abbess, at Argenteuil. When she
became abbess, her community became a centre
of light in France.

Still, Heloise shared the fate of her sisters, if
she had not shared their sin ; in fact, we may

see a protest against their life in her refusal to
follow them to a new home. Suger had been
directed to find a nunnery which would receive
the evicted sisters, and most of them had gone
to St. Mary of Footel. Heloise had not accompanied them, and she was still without a canonical
home in 1129, when the news of these events
reached the distant abbey of St. Gildas.

The finest and supreme test of love is to
purge it of the last subtle admixture of sexual
feeling and then measure its strength. As a
rule this is wholly impracticable—Mr. W. Platt
has a remarkable paper on the subject in his
Women, Love, and Life—but in the case of
Abélard the test was applied in supreme rigour,
and with a satisfactory issue. There was indeed
another consideration impelling Abélard, when he
sought out his nun-wife. The desertion of the
Paraclete had cost him many a heavy thought.
The little estate was still his legal property,
but it was insufficient to support a priest and
companion at the oratory. He would assuage
both anxieties by installing Heloise and such
companions as she chose in his old home. But
the course of the story will reveal more clearly
the deep affection he had for Heloise. It was

faithfulness to the views he held since his conversion, faithfulness to the ideal of the best men
of the time, as well as a dread of the ever ready
tongue of the calumniator, that separated him so
long and so sternly from her.

In 1129, therefore, the year in which the
plague ravaged Paris, Abélard revisited the quiet
valley of the Arduzon. Thither he invited
Heloise and some of her companions, to whom
he made over the legal possession of the estate.
Poor Heloise must have been disappointed. The
ardour which she reveals in her letters was
evidently met by a great restraint and formality
on his side. He was severely correct in the
necessary intercourse with his 'sisters in religion.'
Later events showed that, ridiculous as it may
well seem, he had good reason for this deference
to detractors. However, Heloise soon won universal regard and affection in Champagne. 'The
bishops came to love her as a daughter,' says
Abélard, 'the abbots as a sister, and the laity as
a mother.' They lived in deep poverty and some
anxiety at first, but nobles and prelates soon
added generously to the resources of the new
foundation. Noble dames, too, brought rich
dowries with them in coming to ask for the veil

in Heloise's respected community.   The priory grew rapidly in importance and good repute.

In 1131 Abélard sought a further favour for the new foundation, in having Heloise raised to the dignity of abbess.   Innocent II. was making a journey through France, and lavishing favours (when they cost him nothing) generously and gratuitously on all sides, behaving in a manner that departed widely from papal traditions.   It was the second year of the great papal schism, and, Anacletus having bought or otherwise secured Rome, through his family, the Pierleoni, Innocent was making a successful bid for France, where exception was taken to Pierleone's Jewish strain. Passing from Chartres to Liége, on his way to meet Lothair of Saxony, Innocent spent a day or two at the Benedictine abbey of Morigni. Abélard joined the crowd of prelates who assembled there to do homage to the pope, and he obtained the promise of a bull (which was duly sent), conferring the dignity of abbess on Heloise, and securing to her and her successors the full canonical rights of their abbey.   Abélard seems to have been received with distinction by the papal court.   The chronicle of Morigni mentions the presence of the Abbot of St. Gildas, and adds : 'the most distinguished teacher and master in the schools, to whom lovers of learning flocked from almost the whole of Christendom.' Later, too, Abélard boasts (so says Bernard) of his friends amongst the Roman cardinals ; it must have been during the stay of the papal court at Morigni that he met them. Another noteworthy personage whom Abélard met there was St. Bernard. We have no details about this first meeting of the two great antagonists, but their names occur side by side in the chronicle as those of the most eminent teacher and the most distinguished preacher in France.

In the increasing bitterness of life at St. Gildas Abélard now naturally sought consolation in the new abbey of the Paraclete. His relation to Heloise personally remained marked by a reserve which hurt her, but his visits to the abbey became more frequent and prolonged. It appears that this loosened the tongues of some foolish people, and Abélard took up the accusation, or insinuation, with his usual gravity. His apology is often described as 'ridiculous' and 'painful' ; and one certainly cannot take very seriously his dissertation on Origen's misdeed and the Oriental custom of eunuch-guardians. More interesting is the

second part, in which he urges many precedents
of the familiarity of saintly men with women.
His favourite saint, Jerome, afforded a con-
spicuous illustration ; and others were not wanting.   It is too early in the history of theology
to find the example of Christ adduced.   A
modern apologist could greatly extend the list,
beginning with Francis of Assisi (and Clare) and
ending with Francis de Sales (and Madame de
Chantal).   Perhaps Abélard's own case is the
clearest proof that even masked sexual feeling
may be entirely absent from such attachments.
Those who care to analyse them will probably
find the greater refinement, gentleness, sympathy,
and admiration of women to be quite adequate
to explain such saintly intimacies, without any
subtle research into the psychology of sex.   However, the complaint seems to have moderated the
abbot's fervour for a time ; and indeed events
soon became absorbingly interesting at St. Gildas.

The frequent journeys to Champagne increased
the bitterness of his monks.   Then he had a
serious accident, nearly breaking his neck in a
fall from his horse.   When he recovered, he
found that his monks had entered upon a most
dangerous stage of conspiracy.   The accident

seems to have suggested an idea to them, and they determined to rid themselves of an abbot who was worse than useless. They even put poison in the wine which he was to use in the Mass one morning, but he discovered the fact in time. On another occasion he had an adventure which may have suggested an important incident in M. Zola's *Rome*. He had gone to Nantes to visit the count in an illness, and was staying with his brother Dagobert, who was a canon in the cathedral. When the time came for the abbot and his monastic companion to sup, Abélard had, providentially, lost his appetite —or suspected something. The monk supped— and died. As Abélard's servant disappeared after the meal, it was natural to suppose that he had been paid by the ferocious monks to poison their abbot. ' How many times did they try to do away with me by poison ! ' he exclaimed. But he lived apart from them, and succeeded in frustrating the attempt. Then they hired robbers to apply their professional skill to the task. Whenever the monks heard that he was going anywhere, they planted a few cut-throats on the route.

Abélard had no great love for this Dionysiac existence, and he resolved to make a bold effort at reform. He summoned the monks in solemn chapter, and hurled the sentence of excommunication at the leaders of the revolt. It sat more lightly on their shoulders than the abbot anticipated, and he proceeded to call in the help of a papal legate. The Duke of Brittany and several neighbouring bishops were invited to the function, and the sentence of excommunication and expulsion from the abbey was repeated with impressive ceremony. The chief rebels were thus restricted to following the abbot's movements without—in company, apparently, of the hired assassins of the monks and the equally dangerous servants of the lord of the manor—and Abélard devoted his attention to reforming the remainder of the community. But the old abbey was past redemption. 'The remaining monks began to talk, not of poison, but of cutting my throat,' he says. The circle of knives was drawing closer upon him, within and without, and he saw that it would be impossible to guard his life much longer. He gave up the struggle, and fled from the abbey. There is a local tradition which tells of a secret flight by night through a subterranean passage leading down to the sea. Abélard at least intimates there was little dignity in his retirement, when he says: 'under the guidance of a certain noble of the district I succeeded, with great difficulty, in escaping from the abbey.'

Where Abélard found refuge from his murderous 'sons,' and where he spent the next three or four years, it is difficult to say. He probably moved from place to place, generally remaining in the neighbourhood of Rhuys, but occasionally journeying to Champagne or accepting an invitation to preach at some special festival. The 'certain noble'—an uncertain one, as the phrase usually implies—would be likely to give him immediate hospitality; and the Count of Nantes was friendly, and would find Abélard a graceful addition at his board. Then there was the family château at Pallet, and the house of his brother Dagobert at Nantes. We seem to find Abélard's boy, Astrolabe, under the care of this brother later on. Abélard would at all events see much of him, and assist in educating him, either at Pallet or Nantes. The son had, apparently, not inherited the gifts of his parents. An obscure mention of his death in a later *necrologium* merely indicates the close of a correct but ordinary ecclesiastical career.

But though Abélard lacked neither wealth, nor

honour, nor home, he speaks of his condition as a very pitiable one. Deutsch has hazarded the conjecture that the monks of St. Gildas really desired an abbot who would be generally absent. It seems rather that they wanted an abbot who would share their comfortable theory of life and at the same time have influence to enrich the abbey, discontinue the paying of tribute, and induce a higher authority to restrain their tyrannical neighbours. They were therefore naturally inflamed when Abélard deserted the immediate concerns of the abbey, yet remained near enough to secure his revenue out of its income. He retained his title (we find no successor appointed until after his death), and as he speaks of wealth, we must suppose that he somehow continued to obtain his income. The Count of Nantes would probably support his cause as long as he remained in Brittany. But, at the same time, this detained him in the constant danger of assassination. Wherever he went, he apprehended bribery and corruption, poison and poniards. 'My misery grew with my wealth,' he says, and 'I find no place where I may rest or live.' His classical reading promptly suggests the parallel of Damocles.

It was in these circumstances that Abélard wrote

the famous letter which he entitled the 'Story of my Calamities.' The passage I have just quoted occurs in its closing paragraph. It is an invaluable document for the purpose of the great master's biography. Without it, the life of Abélard would occupy only a score of pages. His contemporaries had numbers of monastic followers and admirers who were eager to write their deeds in letters of gold. The little band of friends who stood around Abélard in his final struggle were scattered, cowed, or murdered, by triumphant Bernardism. At the mention of Bernard's name Christendom crossed itself and raised its eyes to the clouds: at the mention of the 'Peripatetic of Pallet' it closed its pious lips, forgetful, or ignorant, of the twenty years of profound sorrow for the one grave delinquency of his life. If the sins of youth are to leave an indelible stain, one is forced to recall that Augustine had been a greater sinner, and that the Canon of the Church contains the names of converted prostitutes, such as Mary of Magdala and Mary Magdalene of Pazzi. It may be thought by some Catholics that, in the uncertainty of human judgment, there is a providential criterion given in the working of miracles; but, once more, even the fifth century only credited

St. Augustine with two miracles.   And if intention to serve the Church be all-important, Abélard has won high merit ; or if effective service to the Church, then is his merit the greater, for the thirteenth century, in its construction of that theology and philosophy which the Church even now deems sufficient for the needs of the world, utterly rejected Bernardism, and borrowed its foundation from Pierre Abélard.

As a piece of literature the 'Story' lies under the disadvantage of being written in degenerate Latin.   With all his classical reading, Abélard has not escaped the use of forms which gravely offend the classical taste.   Perhaps John of Salisbury is superior to him in this respect ; there have certainly been later theologians, such as Petavius, who have far surpassed him.   But, apart from this limitation in form, it is as high above the many biographies and autobiographies of his contemporaries as he himself was above most of their writers.   Abbot Suger's autobiography is a piece of vulgar and crude self-advertisement beside it. It has not the mere chance immortality which honours such works as that of Suger, and which is wholly due to the zeal of the modern collector of ancient documents ; it has the germ of immortality within it—the same soul that lives in the *Confessions* of Augustine: those who understand that soul will not add the *Confession* of Rousseau. And the confession of Abélard has this singular feature: it is written by a man to whom the former sinful self is dead in a way which was impossible to Augustine. That feature implies both advantages and disadvantages, but it at least gives a unique value and interest to the document.

We have throughout relied on and quoted this autobiography, so that an analysis of its contents would be superfluous. There remains, however, the interesting question of Abélard's motive for writing it. It is ostensibly written as a letter, addressed to a friend who is in trouble, and merely intended to give him some consolation by a comparison of the sorrows of Abélard. No one will seriously question that this is only a rhetorical artifice. Probably it reached such a friend, but it was obviously written for 'publication.' In its sincere acknowledgment of whatever fault lay on his conscience, only striving to excuse where the intention was clearly good, that is, in the matter of his theological opinions, the letter must be regarded as a conciliatory document. Not only its elaborate construction, but its care in explaining how guiltless he was in the making of most of his enemies—Anselm, Alberic, Norbert, Bernard, and the monks of St. Denis and St. Gildas—impel us to think that it was intended for circulation in France. In a few years we shall find him in Paris once more. Deutsch believes that the 'Story' was written and circulated to prepare the way for his return, and this seems very probable. From 'the ends of the earth' his thoughts and hopes were being redirected towards Paris ; it had availed him nothing to fly from it. But there were calumnious versions abroad of every step in his eventful life, and even Bernard sneered at his experience at St. Gildas. He would make an effort to regain the affection of some of his old friends, or to create new admirers.

Whatever may have been the aim of Abélard in writing his 'Story,' it had one immediate consequence of the first literary importance. Great of itself, it evoked a correspondence which is unique in the literature of the world. It fell into the hands of Abbess Heloise, and led to the writing of her famous *Letters*.

CHAPTER XI

THE LETTERS OF ABÉLARD AND HELOISE

THE true interest of the correspondence between the abbot husband and the abbess wife, which resulted from the publication of the 'Story of my Calamities,' needs to be pointed out afresh at the beginning of the twentieth century. It has been obscured through the eagerness of historians to indicate parallels and the tendency of poets and romancers to isolate features which appeal to them. During the eighteenth century the famous letters were made familiar to English readers by a number of translations from the French or from the original Latin. Even then there was a tendency to read them apart from the lives of the writers, or at least without an adequate preliminary study of their characters and their fortunes. Those translations are read no longer. Apart from the limited number of readers who have appreciated the excellent French versions of Madame Guizot and M. Gréard, an idea is formed of the letters and their writers from a few ardent fragments, which are misleading in their isolation, and from the transference of the names 'Abélard' and 'Heloise' to more recent characters of history or romance. The letters must be read anew in the light of our augmented knowledge and of the juster psychological analysis which it has made possible.

There are those whose sole knowledge of Heloise is derived from the reading of Pope's well-known poem, which is taken to be a metrical exposition of her first letter. With such an impression, and a few broad outlines of the life of the lovers, one is well prepared to accept the assertion of a parallel with the *Portuguese Letters* and other of the *lettres amoureuses* which were so dear to the eighteenth century. Probably few who compare Pope with the original, or indeed read him without comparison, will agree with Hallam that he has put 'the sentiments of a coarse and abandoned woman into her mouth.' Johnson found 'no crudeness of sense, no asperity of language' in Pope's poem. Yet no one who has carefully read the original will fail to perceive that Pope has given a greatly distorted version of it. French versifiers found it ' un amusement littéraire et galant,' as has been said of Bussy-Rabutin's version, to isolate the element of passion in the finer soul of Heloise, and thus present her as a twelfth-century Marianne Alcoforado. Pope has yielded somewhat to the same spirit. He does indeed introduce the intellectual judgment and the complex ethical feeling of Heloise in his poem, but he alters the proportions of the psychic elements in her letter, and prepares the way for a false estimate. Pope's *Heloise* is framed in the eighteenth century as naturally as the real *Heloise* is in the twelfth. Still, it must be remembered that Pope did not write from the original Latin letters. He evidently used some of the so-called ' translations,' but really paraphrases, of his time.[1]

The charge must also be laid, though with less insistence, against the parallels which some writers

[1] Mr. Leslie Stephen has kindly drawn my attention to Elwin's theory (Pope's Works) that he followed the translation of J. Hughes, author of the *Siege of Damascus*. Hughes's ' translation ' was little more faithful than the current French versions ; it is largely a work of imagination. Careful comparison does seem to show that Pope used this version, but he seems also to have used some of the very misleading French paraphrases. Elwin himself thinks Pope did not look at the original Latin.

have discovered, or invented, for Heloise. The most famous are the *Portuguese Letters*, a series of singularly ardent love-letters from a Portuguese nun to a French noble. The correspondents are said to have been Marianne Alcoforado and M. de Chamilly—to look at whom, said St. Simon, you would never have thought him the soul of the *Portuguese Letters*. He was neither talented nor handsome, and his liaison with the nun seems to have been no more than the usual temporary incident in a soldier's life. When he returned to France she wrote the letters which are so frequently associated with those of Heloise. It is an unworthy and a superficial comparison. There is a ground for comparison in the condition of the writer and in the free and vivid expression of a consuming love, but they are separated by profound differences. The Portuguese nun has nothing but her love; her life is being consumed in one flame of passion. Heloise is never so wholly lost in her passion; she can regard it objectively. Even were Abélard other than he was at the time, no one who knows Heloise could conceive her, after her vows, to say, 'if it were possible for me to get out of this miserable cloister, I should not wait in Portugal for the fulfilment of your promise,' or imagine her, under any conditions, to talk lightheartedly to her lover of 'the languid pleasures your French mistresses give you,' and remind him that he only sought in her 'un plaisir grossier.' There is not a word, in any of the *Portuguese Letters*, of God, of religious vows, of any thought or feeling above the plane of sense, of any appreciation of the literal sacrilege of her position, of anything but a wilful abandonment to a violent passion.

There are the same defects, though they are less obtrusive, in the parallel which Rousseau claimed in giving the title of the *Nouvelle Heloïse* to his Savoyard letters. The accidental resemblance of the religious costume is wanting here, but, on the other hand, there is a greater show of character. Rousseau has confused the Heloise of 1117 and the abbess of the letters. From another point of view, one would like to know what Bussy-Rabutin or Colardeau would have thought of the *Nouvelle Heloïse* as the expression of an absorbing passion. Rousseau, who held that the *Portuguese Letters* had been written by a man, was of the singular opinion that no woman could describe, or even feel, love. The letters of his Julie are pale fires beside the first and second letters of Heloise.[1]

In direct opposition to the writers who find parallels for the correspondence of abbess and abbot we have a few critics who deny or doubt the authenticity of the letters. It is significant that the recent and critical German biographers of Abélard do not even mention these doubts. They have, in truth, the slenderest of foundations. Lalanne, who has endeavoured to spread this heresy in faithful France, can say little more than that he cannot reconcile the tone of the letters with the age and condition of the writers; he also says that Abélard would be hardly likely to preserve such letters had he received them from his wife. Orelli has tried to sow similar doubts in the apparently more promising soil of German culture, but with no greater success. If it seems incredible that Heloise should have penned the letters which bear her name, how shall we qualify the supposition that there lived, some time within

---

[1] I hardly like to speak of the feeble creation of Robert Buchanan in such a company, but his 'New Abélard' is a further illustration. His pitiful Mr. Bradley has no earthly resemblance to Abélard, except in a most superficial sense. It is grotesque to compare him to Abélard for his 'heresy'; and to say that he recalls Abélard in his weakness (to the extent of bigamously marrying and blasting the life of a noble woman) is deeply unjust. Abélard was not a cad.

the following century, a genius capable of creating them, yet utterly unknown to his contemporaries? If they are the work of some admirer of Abélard, as Orelli thinks, they reveal a higher literary competency than Rousseau shows in his *Nouvelle Heloïse*. We are asked to reject a wonder in the name of a greater wonder. Moreover, an admirer of Abélard would not have written the letters which bear his name in a style that has won for him anything but the admiration of posterity. And it is quite impossible to admit one series of the letters without the other.

Setting apart the letters of Abélard, which it is idle to question in themselves, it must be admitted that there are features in the letters of Heloise which are startling to the modern mind. These are the features on which her romantic admirers have concentrated ; they will appear in due course. But when one evades the pressure of modern associations, and considers the correspondence in its twelfth-century setting, there is no inherent improbability in it. Rather the reverse. As to the publication of letters in which husband and wife had written the most sacred confidences, we need not suppose, as M. Gréard does, that Heloise ever intended such a result, or built up her notes into letters for that purpose. Nothing compels us to think that they were brought together until years after the writers had been laid in a common tomb. There are obvious interpolations, it is true, but we shall only increase the difficulty—nay, we shall create a difficulty— if we look upon the most extraordinary passages in the letters as coming from any other source than the heart of an impassioned lover.

As regards what a logician would call the external difficulty—that we cannot trace the letters further back than the middle of the thirteenth century—it need not discompose us. The conditions which make a negative argument of that character valid are not present here. Abélard had been condemned and his party scattered. There are no writers to whom we should look for allusions to the letters before Guillaume de Lorris and Jehan le Meung manifestly introduce them in the *Roman de la Rose*. Indeed this circumstance, and the fact that the oldest manuscript we have dates from one hundred years after the death of Heloise, incline one to think that she wished the treasure to be preserved in a reverent privacy.

To give any large proportion of the letters

here would be impossible, yet we must give such extracts from them as may serve in the task of reconstructing character. It was an age when the practice, if not the art, of letter-writing greatly flourished. St. Bernard's letters form a portly and a remarkable volume. The chroniclers of the time have preserved an immense number of the Latin epistles which busy couriers bore over the land. One is prepared, therefore, to find much formality, much attention to the rules and the conventional graces of the epistolary art, even in the letters of Heloise. The strong, impetuous spirit does at times break forth, in splendid violence, from its self-imposed restraint, but we have, on the whole, something very unlike the utter and unthinking outpouring of an ebullient passion which is found in the letters of the Portuguese nun. Arguments are rounded with quotations from classic writers ; dialectical forms are introduced here and there ; a care for literary manner and construction of the Latin periods is manifested. Bayle says her Latin is 'too frequently pedantic and subtile.' It is, at all events, much superior to the average Latinity of the time, though, as in the case of Abélard, the characteristic defects of this are not entirely avoided.

Some day, then, after his 'Story' had gone forth on its peaceful mission into France, Abélard received a folded parchment in the once familiar hand.

'To her lord, yea father : to her spouse, yea brother : from his servant, yea daughter—his wife, his sister : to Abélard from Heloise.'

So ran the superscription, a curious effort to breathe life into a formality of the day. Chance has brought to their abbey, she says, a copy of the letter he has recently sent forth. The story of his saddened life and of the dangers that yet multiply about him has affected them so deeply that they are filled with anxiety for him. 'In hourly anguish do our trembling hearts and heaving breasts await the dread rumour of thy death. By Him who still extends to thee an uncertain protection we implore thee to inform us, His servants and thine, by frequent letter, of the course of the storms in which thou art still tossed ; so that thou mayst let us at least, who have remained true to thee, share thy sorrow or thy joy. And if the storm shall have abated somewhat, so much the more speedily do thou send us an epistle which will bring so much joy to us.' She invokes the authority of Seneca on the epistolary duties of friends, and she has a holier claim than that of friend, a stronger one than that of wife. 'At thy command I would change, not merely my costume, but my very soul, so entirely art thou the sole possessor of my body and my spirit. Never, God is my witness, never have I sought anything in thee but thyself : I have sought thee, not thy gifts. I have not looked to the marriage bond or dowry : I have not even yearned to satisfy my own will and pleasure, but thine, as thou well knowest. The name of wife may be the holier and more approved, but the name of friend—nay, mistress or concubine, if thou wilt suffer it—has always been the sweeter to me. For in thus humbling myself for thee, I should win greater favour from thee, and do less injury to thy greatness. This thou hast thyself not wholly forgotten, in the aforesaid letter thou hast written for the consolation of a friend. Therein also thou hast related some of the arguments with which I essayed to turn thee from the thought of our unhappy wedlock, though thou hast omitted many in which I set forth the advantage of love over matrimony, freedom over bondage. God is my witness that if Augustus, the emperor of the whole world, were

to honour me with the thought of wedlock, and
yield me the empire of the universe, I should
deem it more precious and more honourable to be
thy mistress than to be the queen of a Cæsar.'

She claims no merit for her devotion. Abélard's
greatness more than justifies her seeming extravagance. 'Who,' she asks, going back to his
golden age, 'who did not hasten forth to look
as thou didst walk abroad, or did not follow thee
with outstretched neck and staring eyes? What
wife, what maid, did not yearn for thee? What
queen or noble dame was there who did not envy
my fortune?'

Yet she would ask this measure of gratitude
from him, that he write to her at times. He
had never known refusal from her. 'It was not
religious fervour that drew me to the rigour of
the conventual life, but thy command. How
fruitlessly have I obeyed, if this gives me no title
to thy gratitude! . . . When thou didst hasten
to dedicate thyself to God I followed thee—nay,
I went before thee. For, as if mindful of the
looking back of Lot's wife, thou didst devote me
to God before thyself, by the sacred habit and
vows of the monastery. Indeed it was in this
sole circumstance that I had the sorrow and the

shame of noting thy lack of confidence in me.
God knows that I should not have hesitated a
moment to go before or to follow thee to the
very gates of hell, hadst thou commanded it. My
soul was not my own but thine.'

Let him, therefore, make this small return of a
letter to relieve her anxiety. 'In earlier days,
when thou didst seek worldly pleasure with me,
thy letters were frequent enough ; thy songs put
the name of Heloise on every lip. Every street,
every house in the city, echoed with my name.
How juster would it be to lead me now to God
than thou then didst to pleasure ! Think then, I
beseech thee, how much thou owest me. With
this brief conclusion I terminate my long letter.
Farewell, beloved.'

It is small wonder that the epistle placed Abélard
in some perplexity. True, the devoted Heloise
had spoken throughout in the past tense. But
the ardour and the violence of her phrases betrayed a present depth of emotion which he must
regard with some dismay. He had trusted that
time and discipline would subdue the flame he
had enkindled, and here it was indirectly revealed
to live still in wondrous strength. He could not
refuse to write, nor indeed would such a neglect

profit anything ; but he would send her a long
letter of spiritual direction, and endeavour to
divert her meditations.

'To Heloise, his sister in Christ, from Abélard,
her brother in Him,' was the characteristic opening
of his reply. If he has not written to her since
her conversion, he says, it is not from neglect nor
want of affection, but from the thought that she
needed neither counsel nor consolation. She had
been prioress at Argenteuil, the consoler and in-
structor of others. Yet, 'if it seems otherwise to
thy humility,' he will certainly write her on any
point she may suggest. She has spoken of prayer,
and so he diverges into a long dissertation on the
excellence of prayer, which fills nearly the whole
of his pages. On one or two occasions only does
he approach that colloquy of soul to soul, for
which Heloise yearned so ardently. 'We ourselves are united not only by the sanctity of our
oath, but also by the identity of our religious
profession. I will pass over your holy community,
in which the prayers of so many virgins and
widows ever mount up to God, and speak of thee
thyself, whose holiness hath much favour with
God, I doubt not, and remind thee what thou
owest me, particularly in this grievous peril of

mine.   Do thou remember, then, in thy prayers
him who is so specially thine own.'   And when
at length he nears the end of his edifying treatise,
he once more bares the heart that still beats within
him.   If, he says, they hear before long that he
has fallen a victim to the plots of his enemies, or
has by some other chance laid down his burden of
sorrow, he trusts they will have his body brought
to rest in their home, his own dear Paraclete, 'for
there is no safer and more blessed spot for the
rest of a sorrowing soul.'

The long letter is, on the whole, prudent and
formal to a degree.   Yet it is not true that
Abélard had nothing but coldness and prudence
to return to his wife's devotion.   It is quite
obvious what Abélard would conceive to be his
duty in replying to Heloise.   For her sake and
for his, for her happiness and his repute, he must
moderate the threatening fire.   But that he had a
true affection and sympathy for her is made clear
by the occasional failure of his pious resolution.
'Sister, who wert once dear to me in the world
and art now most dear in Christ,' he once exclaims
parenthetically ; and at other moments he calls
her 'dearest sister,' and even 'beloved.'   When
we remember the gulf that now separated them,

besides his obvious duty to guide her, we shall accept the contrast of their letters without using harsh words of the distracted abbot. But the pathos and the humanity of his closing paragraph defeated his purpose, and the whole soul of the abbess flames forth in her reply.

It opens with a calm and somewhat artificial quarrel with the superscription of his letter, but soon breaks out into strong reproach for his talk of death. 'How hast thou been able to frame such thoughts, dearest?' she asks; 'how hast thou found words to convey them?' 'Spare me, beloved,' she says again: 'talk not of death until the dread angel comes near.' Moreover, she and her nuns would be too distracted with grief to pray over his corpse. Seneca and Lucan are quoted to support her. Indeed she soon lapses into words which the theologian would call blasphemous. She turns her face to the heavens with that old, old cry, Where is Thy boasted justice? They were untouched in the days of their sinful joy, but smitten with a thousand sorrows as soon as their bed had the sacramental blessing. 'Oh, if I dared but call God cruel to me! Oh, most wretched of all creatures that I am!' Women have ever been the ruin of men

—Adam, Solomon, Samson, Job—she runs through the long category of man's sneaking accusations.

She wishes she could make satisfaction to God for her sin, but, 'if I must confess the true infirmity of my wretched soul, how can I appease Him, when I am always accusing Him of the deepest cruelty for this affliction?' There is yet a further depth that she must lay bare to her father confessor and her spouse. How can there be question of penance 'when the mind still retains the thought of sinning, and is inflamed again with the old longing? So sweet did I find the pleasures of our loving days, that I cannot bring myself to reject them, nor banish them from my memory. Wheresoever I go they thrust themselves upon my vision, and enkindle the old desire. Even when I sleep they torment me with their fancied joy. Even during the Mass, when our prayer should be purest, the dreadful vision of those pleasures so haunts my soul that I am rather taken up with them than with prayer. I ought to be lamenting what I have done ; I am rather lamenting what I miss. Not only our actions, but the places and the times are so bound up with the thought of thee in my mind, that night and day I am repeating all with thee in spirit. The movement of body reveals my thoughts at times ; they are betrayed in unguarded speech. Oh, woe is me ! . . . Not knowing my hypocrisy, people call me "chaste." They deem bodily integrity a virtue, whereas virtue resides in the mind, not the body.' Moreover, virtue should be practised out of love for God, whereas 'God knows that in every part of my life I have more dread of offending thee than Him ; I have a greater desire to please thee than Him.' Let him not deceive himself with trust in *her* prayers, but rather help her to overcome herself. And the poor woman, the nobility of her soul hidden from her and crushed under the appalling ethical ignorance and perverse ordering of her times, ends with a plaintive hope that she may yet, in spite of all, find some corner in heaven that will save her from the abyss.

We have here the passages which have made Heloise an heroine in erotic circles for so many centuries. On these words, isolated from their context of religious horror and self-accusation, have Bussy-Rabutin, and Pope, and the rest, erected their gaudy structures ; on them is grounded the parallel with Marianne Alcoforado, and Rousseau's Julie, and so many other women

Q

who have meditated sin. Bayle has carried his Pyrrhonism so far as to doubt that 'bodily integrity' which she claims for herself with so little boasting; Chateaubriand, with broader and truer judgment, finds in the letter the mirroring of the soul of a good woman.

There can be little doubt that the optimism of Chateaubriand has for once come nearer to the truth than the cynicism of Bayle. The decadent admirers of Heloise forget three circumstances which should have diminished their equivocal adoration : the letter is from a wife to her husband, from a penitent to her spiritual guide— women say such things every day in the confessional, even in this very sensitive age—from a thoughtful woman to a man whom she knew to be dead to every breath of sensual love. There is no parallel to such a situation.

Further, it is now obvious that the romancists have done injustice to the soul of Heloise in their isolation of her impassioned phrases. She objectifies her love : she is not wholly merged in it. She never loses sight of its true position in her actual life. It is an evil, a temptation, a torment —she would be free from it. Yet she is too rational a thinker to turn to the easy theory of an

outward tempter. It is part of herself, a true
outgrowth of the nature God has given her ; and
between the voice of nature and the voice of
conscience, complicated by the influence of conventual tradition and written law, her soul is rent
with a terrific struggle. A modern confessor with
a knowledge of physiology—there are a few such
—could have led her into paths of peace without
difficulty. There was no sin in her.

It is impossible to say that Abélard sails fault-
lessly through these troubled waters, but his
answer to her on this point is true and sound in
substance. 'God grant that it be so in thy soul
as thou hast written,' he says in his next letter.
It is true that he is chiefly regarding her humility,
and that he does not shed the kindly light of
human wisdom on her soul which an earlier
Abélard would have done ; yet we can imagine
what St. Bernard or Robert d'Arbrissel would
have answered to such an outpouring. However,
apart from the happy moderation of this reply,
Abélard's third letter only increases our sympathy
with this woman who wanders in the desert of the
twelfth century of the Christian era. The wild
cry of the suffering heart has startled him. He
becomes painfully ingenious in defending Provid-

ence and the monastic or Buddhistic view of life. As to his death, why should she be moved so strongly? 'If thou hadst any trust in the divine mercy towards me, the more grievous the afflictions of this life seem to thee the more wouldst thou desire to see me freed from them! Thou knowest of a certainty that whoever will deliver me from this life will deliver me from a heavy penalty. What I may incur hereafter I know not, but there is no uncertainty as to that which I escape.' And again, when he comes to her accusations of Providence: if she would follow him to 'the home of Vulcan,' why cannot she follow him quietly to heaven? As to her saying that God spared them in their guilt and smote them in their wedded innocence, he denies the latter point. They were not innocent. Did they not have conjugal relations in the holy nunnery of the Virgin at Argenteuil?[1] Did he not profanely dress her in the habit of a nun when he took her secretly to Pallet? Flushed with the success of his apology for Providence, the unlucky abbot goes from bathos to bathos. There was not merely justice but love in the

[1] The one from which the nuns had been driven 'on account of the enormity of their life.'

divine ruling. They had merited punishment, but had, ' on the contrary,' been rescued from the ' vile and obscene pleasures' of matrimony, from the ' mud and mire,' and so forth. His mutilation was a skilful operation on the part of Providence ' to remove the root of all vice and sordidness from him, and make him fitter for the service of the altar.' ' I had deserved death, and I have received life. Do thou, then, unite with me in thanksgiving, my inseparable companion, who hast shared both my sin and my reward.' How fortunate it was that they married ! ' For if thou hadst not been joined to me in matrimony, it might easily have happened that thou wouldst have remained in the world '—the one thing that would have saved her from utter desolation. ' Oh, how dread a loss, how lamentable an evil it had been, if in the seeking of carnal pleasure thou hadst borne a few children in pain to the world, whereas thou now bearest so great a progeny with joy to heaven.' Again the ' mud and mire,' and the thanksgiving. He even lends his pen, in his spiritual ecstasy, to the writing of this fearful calumny against himself : ' Christ is thy true lover, not I ; all that I sought in thee was the satisfaction of my miserable pleasure.' Her passions are, like the artificially stimulated ones of the deacons in Gibbon and of Robert d'Arbrissel, a means of martyrdom. He had been spared all this, she had plaintively written ; on the contrary, he urges, she will win more merit and reward than he.

I have given a full summary of the long epistle, because its psychological interest is great. We have seen the gradual transformation of Abélard—the steps in his ' conversion '—from chapter to chapter. This letter marks the deepest stage of his lapse into Bernardism.[1] It offers an almost unprecedented contrast to the Abélard of 1115. And this is the man, I may be pardoned for repeating, who is held up by ecclesiastical writers (even such as Newman) to the blushes of the ages. Perhaps the age is not far off that will sincerely blush over him—not for his personal defects.

Heloise was silenced. Whether the pious dissertation had really influenced her, or the proud utterance of her plaint had relieved her, or she closed in upon her heart after such a reply, it

---

[1] At a later date one of the censures passed by the doctors of the Sorbonne on this classic sinner of the twelfth century is that he finds a shade of sin in legitimate conjugal relations.

would be difficult to say. Her next letter is calm, erudite, dialectical. 'To her lord as to species, her beloved in person' is the quaint heading of the epistle. She will try to keep her pen within due bounds in future, but he knows the saying about 'the fulness of the heart.' Nevertheless, 'just as a nail is driven out by a new one, so it is with thoughts.' He must help her to dwell on other things. She and her nuns beg him to write a new rule for them and a history of the monastic life. There are points in the Rule of St. Benedict which are peculiarly masculine; she discusses them in early mediæval style. She would like her nuns to be permitted to eat meat and drink wine. There is less danger in giving wine to women; and she naïvely quotes (from Macrobius) Aristotle's crude speculation on the subject. Then follows a long dissertation on wine, temperance, and intemperance, bristling with proofs and weighty authorities. Briefly, she quarrels with the ascetic view of life. She happily avoids the hard sayings in which Christ urges it on every page of the Gospels, and voices the eternal compromise of human nature. Who may become Abélard's successor as their spiritual guide, she does not know. Let him appoint a rule of life for them, which will guard them from unwise interference, and let it concede a little in the way of soft clothing, meat, wine, and other suspected commodities.

Abélard complies willingly, quite entering into the spirit of the nail theory. 'I will make a brief and succinct reply to thy affectionate request, dear sister,' he begins, at the head of a very long and very curious sketch of the history of monasticism. It is a brilliant proof of Abélard's erudition, relatively to his opportunities, but at the same time an illustration of the power of constructing most adequate 'explanations' without any reference to the real agencies at work.

In a later letter Abélard drew up the rule of life which had been asked. It follows the usual principles and tendencies of such documents. It offers, however, no little psychological interest in connection with the modifications which the abbess has desired. The dialectician feels a logical reluctance to compromise, and the fervent monk cannot willingly write down half measures. Yet the human element in him has a sneaking sympathy with the plea of the abbess, and, with much explanation and a fond acceptance of Aristotelic theories, the compromise is effected. To the manuscript of this letter a later hand has added a smaller and more practical rule. This is generally attributed to Heloise herself, and is certainly the work of some early abbess of the Paraclete. It supplements Abélard's scheme of principles and general directions by a table of regulations — as to beds, food, dress, visitors, scandals, etc.—of a more detailed character.

The closing letter of the famous series is one addressed by Abélard to 'the virgins of the Paraclete' on the subject of 'the study of letters.' It is from this epistle that we learn—as we do also from a letter of Venerable Peter of Cluny— of Heloise's linguistic acquirements. The nuns are urged to undertake the study of the Scriptural tongues, Latin, Greek, and Hebrew, and are reminded that they have 'a mother who is versed in these three languages.' There is reason to think that neither master nor pupil knew much Greek or Hebrew.

This is followed shortly by a number of hymns and sermons. Heloise had asked him to write some hymns for liturgical use, so as to avoid a wearisome repetition and to dispense with some inappropriate ones. He sent ninety-three, but they are of little literary and poetic value. The source of his old-time poetic faculty is dried up. A sequence for the Feast of the Annunciation, which is attributed to him, won praise from, of all people, Luther. But the number of hymns and songs 'attributed' to Abélard is large. The sermons, of which thirty-four are to be found in the collection of his works, are not distinguished in their order. The abbot was not an eloquent preacher. But they are carefully written, erudite compositions, which were delivered at St. Gildas, or the Paraclete, or by special invitation. Some of them have much intrinsic interest or value— those on Susannah and John the Baptist, for instance, in connection with monastic affairs, and that on St. Peter in connection with his rigid loyalty to Rome.

A more interesting appendix to the correspondence is found in the forty-two 'Problems of Heloise,' with the replies of Abélard. Under the pretext of following out his direction, but probably with a greater anxiety to prolong the intercourse, Heloise sent to him a list of difficulties she had encountered in reading Scripture. The daughters of Charlemagne had responded to Alcuin's exhortations with a similar list. The little treatise is not unworthy of analysis from the historico-theological point of view, but such a task cannot be undertaken here. The problems are, on the whole, those which have presented themselves to every thoughtful man and woman who has approached the Bible with the strictly orthodox view ; the answers are, generally speaking, the theological artifices which served that purpose down to the middle of the wayward nineteenth century.

With this mild outbreak of rationalism Heloise passes out of the pages of history, save for a brief reintroduction in Abélard's closing year. The interest and the force of her personality have been undoubtedly exaggerated by some of the chief biographers of Abélard, but she was assuredly an able, remarkable, and singularly graceful and interesting woman. Cousin once suddenly asked in the middle of a discourse: 'Who is the woman whose love it would have been sweetest to have shared?' Many names were suggested, though there must have been a strong anticipation that he would name Mme. de Longueville, for he laboured at that very time under his posthumous infatuation for the sister of Condé. But he answered, Heloise, 'that noble creature who loved like a St. Theresa, wrote sometimes like

Seneca, and who must have been irresistibly
charming, since she charmed St. Bernard himself.' It was a fine phrase to deliver impromptu,
but an uncritical estimate. It is a characteristic
paradox to say that she loved like a St. Theresa,
and an exaggeration to say that she ever wrote
like Seneca. As to her charming St. Bernard—
the ' pseudo-apostle,' as she ungraciously calls him,
—they who read the one brief letter he wrote her
will have a new idea of a charmed man. Yet
with her remarkable ability, her forceful and
exalted character in the most devitalising circumstances, and her self-realisation, she would probably have written her name in the annals of
France without the assistance of Abélard. It
must be remembered that she had a very singular
reputation, for her age, before she met Abélard.
She might have been a St. Theresa to Peter of
Cluny, or, as is more probable, a Montmorency
in the political chronicle of France.

CHAPTER XII

A RETURN TO THE ARENA

THE literary and personal activity described in
the preceding chapter, together with the elaboration of a new 'theology,' of which we shall read
presently, brings the story of Abélard's life down
to 1135 or 1136.   His movements during the
three or four years after his flight from St. Gildas
are very obscure.   St. Bernard seems to speak
of his presence in Paris at one time, though the
passages can, and perhaps should, be explained
away.   Heloise speaks of his visits to the Paraclete.   On the whole he probably remained in
Brittany, at Nantes or Pallet, and devoted his
time to literary work.   But in 1136 we find him
in Paris once more.   Whether the monks succeeded in making Brittany too insecure for him,
or the count failed to guarantee his income, or a
natural disgust with the situation and longing for
the intellectual arena impelled him to return, we

cannot say. It is only known that in 1136 he was once more quickening the scholastic life of Europe from the familiar slope of St. Genevieve.

So swift and eventful has been the career of the great teacher that one realises with difficulty that he is now almost an old man, a man in his fifty-seventh or fifty-eighth year. It is twenty years since the grim termination of his early Parisian activity, and a new generation fills the schools. The ideas with which he first startled and conquered the intellectual world have been made familiar. The vigour, the freshness, the charming pertinacity of youth have departed. Yet there is no master in Christendom, young or old, that can restrain the flood of 'barbarians' when 'Li mestre' reappears at Paris. John of Salisbury was amongst the crowd. It is from his *Metalogicus* that we first learn of Abélard's return to the arena, and the renewal of his old triumph. St. Bernard fully confirms the story, after his fashion. Indeed, in one sense Abélard's triumph was greater than ever, for he gathered a notable group of followers about him on St. Genevieve. There was Arnold of Brescia, the scourge of the Italian clergy, the 'gad-fly' of the hierarchy. There was Gilbert de la Porée, a dreaded dialec-

tician and rationalistic theologian.   There was
Hyacinth, the young deacon and noble from
Rome, afterwards a power in the sacred college.
There was Bérenger, the caustic critic, who gave
Bernard many an unpleasant quarter of an hour.
There were future bishops and theologians in
remarkable numbers.

However, we have no information of a definite
character until five years afterwards.   In fact
John of Salisbury complicates the situation by
stating that Abélard withdrew shortly after 1136.
Deutsch thinks that Abélard left Paris for a few
years; Hausrath, on the contrary, conjectures
that he merely changed the locality of his school.
John of Salisbury would, in that case, have
followed his lectures in the cloistral school in
1136, and would have remained faithful to the
abbey, following Abélard's successor, a Master
Alberic, when Abélard was, for some unknown
reason, constrained to move his chair to the
chapel of St. Hilary, also on the slope of St.
Genevieve.   According to the *Historia Pontificalis* it was at St. Hilary that Bernard visited
him in 1141.   It is an ingenious way of keeping
Abélard in Paris during the five years, as most
historians would prefer to do.   Its weak point is

the supposition that John of Salisbury would continue to attend at the abbey of St. Genevieve with Abélard teaching a few yards away.

The difficulty may be gladly left to the chronologist. The first great fact in Abélard's career after his return to Paris is that St. Bernard begins to take an active interest in his teaching in the spring of 1141. Ten short weeks afterwards the prestige of the great teacher was shattered beyond recall, and he set out upon his pathetic journey to the tomb. It was a tense, a titanic struggle, on the side of Bernard.

According to the religious story-books the episode is very clear and highly honourable to Bernard. Abbot Abélard had rewritten, with what he thought to be emendations, the theological treatise which had been burnt at Soissons. Under the title of the *Theologia Christiana*, this rationalistic exposition and defence of the dogmas of the faith, especially of the Trinity, had 'crossed the seas and leaped over the Alps,' in Bernard's vivid phraseology. With it travelled also an *Introductio ad Theologiam*, which was written soon after it, and his *Commentary on the Epistle to the Romans*, of earlier date. The books we have previously mentioned, the *Sic et Non*, and the *Ethics* or *Know Thyself*, had a more limited and secluded circulation. The theological work which has the title of *Epitome Theologiae Christianae* or *Sententiae Petri Abaelardi* is considered by most experts to be a collection of his opinions drawn up by some other masters for scholastic use.[1]

The story runs that these works chanced to intrude on the pious meditations of a mystic theologian of the name of William of St. Thierry. William was very nearly a saint, and the new theology shocked him inexpressibly. He had been abbot of St. Thierry at Rheims, but had been elevated from the Benedictine level to the Cistercian under Bernard's influence, and was peacefully composing a commentary on the highly mystical 'Song of Songs,' in the Cistercian monastery at Signy, when Abélard's heresies reached him.[2] In his horror he selected thirteen definite heretical

---

[1] It is quite beside the writer's purpose, and probably the reader's pleasure, to give an analysis of these works. I shall presently treat the specific points that have relation to his condemnation, and I add a supplementary chapter on his teaching in general. Deutsch may be read by the curious, and Herr Hausrath gives a useful shorter analysis.

[2] A good idea of the man, and of the rapidly growing school he belonged to, will be formed from the opening sentence of one of his treatises: 'Rotting in the lake of misery and in the mire of filth,

statements from the books, and sent them, with the treatises, to his pious and powerful friend, Bernard of Clairvaux, with a pressing request to examine them and take action. Bernard replied that a cursory perusal of the books seemed to justify his follower's zeal. He would put the matter aside until after Holy Week, then talk it over with William. In the meantime William must bear patiently with his inactivity, since he 'had hitherto known little or nothing of these things.' Easter over, and the conference having presumably taken place, Bernard was convinced of Abélard's errors. Faithful to Christ's direction, he went up to Paris, and personally reproved his erring brother, without witnesses. Bernard's biographer (and secretary-monk) assures that Abélard promised to amend his ways. The amendment not taking place, Bernard paid him a second brotherly visit, and, as he refused to comply, Bernard followed out the evangelical direction of reproving him before others. He attacked him in the presence of his students, warning the latter that they must burn his heretical writings forth-

and stuck in the mud of the abyss that has no substance, and from the depths of my grief, I cry out to Thee, O Lord.' He was in the midst of a similar Bernardesque composition when he received Abelard's works.

with. It is one of the scenes in Abélard's career which it would have been interesting to have witnessed.

However, we must defer for a moment the continuation of the Bernardist version of the encounter, and examine the course of events more critically.

The theory that St. Bernard had not occupied himself with the errors of Abélard until William of St. Thierry drew his attention to them is a very poor and foolish composition. We could as well imagine that Newman knew 'little or nothing' of Dr. Arnold's views in the early thirties. Bernard and Abélard had been for many years the supreme representatives of the new 'High' and 'Broad' movements of the twelfth century; and Bernard had a far more intense dread of rationalism than Newman. Scarcely an event of moderate importance occurred in Church, school, or state, in France at least, that escaped the eye of the abbot of Clairvaux in those days. He was 'acting-Pope' to the Church of Christ, and he felt all the responsibility. And, amongst the multitudinous cares of his office, none gave him greater concern than the purity of the faith and the purification of the disquieting scholastic activity of the day.

We have seen in a former chapter how largely antithetic his position was to that of Abélard, and that he was a man who could not doubt for a moment the truth of his own conception of religion. There was the same marked antithesis at the very bases of their theological conceptions, in the mental soil in which those conceptions took root. Bernard was more authoritative than Anselm of Laon, more mystic than Anselm of Canterbury. He had gone further than Anselm on the theory that ' faith precedes reason ' ; Abélard had gone beyond Roscelin with the inverse proposition. Perhaps Bernard's commentary on the ' Song of Songs ' furnishes the best illustration of his frame of mind and his outlook. Towards the close of his life he devoted himself to long and profound meditation on that beautiful piece of Oriental literature. We must not forget, of course, that the Church is largely responsible for his extravagance on this point. It has indeed taken the civilisation of the West more than two thousand years to discover that its glowing verses are inspired only by the rounded limbs and sweet breath of a beautiful woman ; and its most erotic passages are still solemnly applied to the Mother of Christ on her annual festivals. But Bernard revelled in

its 'mystic' phrases.   Day by day, for more than
a year, he gathered his monks about him in the
auditorium at Clairvaux, and expounded to them
the profound spiritual meanings of the 'Song.'
Eighty-three long sermons barely exhausted the
first two chapters.   In the end he devoted three
lengthy discourses, on successive days, to the
elucidation of the words : 'In my bed at night
I have longed for him whom my soul loveth.'

This mystic and unreasoning attitude brought
him into fundamental antagonism with Abélard.
To him faith was the soul's first duty ; reason
might think itself fortunate if there were crumbs
of knowledge in the accepted writings which it
could digest.   To reason, to ask a question, was
honestly incomprehensible and abhorrent to him.
He insisted that the rationalist told God he would
not accept what he could not understand ; whereas
the rationalist was prevented by his own logic
from questioning the veracity of the Infinite, and
merely insisted that, in a world of hallucination
and false pretence, it were well to make sure
that the proposition in question really did come
from God.   Bernard thought reasoning about the
Trinity implied irreverence or incredulity ; Abélard
felt it to be a high service to divine truth, in pre-

paring it for minds which were not blessed with
the mystic sense. Bernard believed Christ died
purely and crudely to make amends to the Father;
Abélard thought this would impute vindictiveness
to God. And so on through a long list of dogmatic points which were of unspeakable importance
in the eyes of the twelfth century.

A conflict was inevitable. In Bernard's thought
Abélard was employing an extraordinary ability to
the grave prejudice of the honour of God, the
safety of the Church, and the supreme interest
of humanity. Bernard would have deserted his
principles and his clear subjective duty if he had
remained silent. If he had 'a quick ear' to catch
'the distant thunder roll of free inquiry,' as Cotter
Morison says, and no one questions, he must have
turned his zealous attention to Abélard long ago,
as we have already seen. But the rationalist had
been rendered powerless in Brittany for some
years. Now that he was teaching with great
effectiveness at Paris once more, Bernard could
not but take action.

However, it is a task of extreme difficulty for
an impartial student to trace with confidence the
early stages of that memorable conflict. We
have seen the Bernardist version; the version of

some of the recent biographers of Abélard is very different. Deutsch and Hausrath, able and critical scholars, believe that the letter from William of St. Thierry had been written, wholly or in part, by Bernard himself; that Bernard's reply was part of a comedy of intrigue; that a timid and treacherous conventicle of the Cistercian monks, including Bernard, had deliberately drawn up in advance this equivocal plan of campaign. Now, if the Catholic enthusiast is incapable of dealing quite impartially with such a problem, it is equally certain that the heretic has a similar disturbing element in his natural predilection for picking holes in the coats of the canonised. The evidence must be examined very carefully. The presumption is that a man of the exalted idealism and stern self-discipline of St. Bernard would not lend himself to such manœuvres. Yet these things are not inconsistent with the dignity of canonisation; moreover, the object was a great and holy one—and Bernard had a mortal dread of the dialectician.

In the first place, then, it is impossible to credit Bernard with the whole of the letter which bears the name of William of St. Thierry. Much of it is by no means Bernardesque in style and manner;

and there are passages which it is quite impossible, on moral grounds, to conceive as having been written by Bernard himself. At the same time much of it does certainly seem to have been written by Bernard. There are few better judges of such a point than Deutsch. The contention that William would not have dared to address such a demand simultaneously to Bernard and Geoffrey without instructions is more precarious.

On the other hand, the letter seems in many respects to support the idea of a diplomatic arrangement. It is addressed to Bernard and to Geoffrey of Chartres, and opens as follows : 'God knows that I am filled with confusion, my lords and fathers, when I am constrained to address you, insignificant as I am, on a matter of grave urgency, since you and others whose duty it is to speak remain silent.' After a little of this strain he recounts how he 'lately chanced to read a certain work' of the dreadful heretic he has named—the *Theology of Peter Abélard*. From it he selects thirteen heretical propositions (we shall meet them later), which he submits to their judgment. If they also condemn, he calls for prompt and effective action. 'God knows that I too have loved him' [Abélard], he says, 'and would remain in charity with him, but in such a cause as this I know no friend or acquaintance.' Finally, he says : 'There are, I am told, other works of his, the *Sic et Non* and the *Scito te Ipsum*, and others . . . but I am told that they shun the light, and cannot be found.'

Without straining an impressionist argument, it may be at once pointed out that the letter betrays itself. Several of the propositions in the list are not found in either of Abélard's theologies ; they are taken from the works which William affirms he has never seen. An intrigue is revealed ; some other person, not at Signy, has had an important share in the epistle, if not in the actual writing of it. Again, as Neander says in his *Life of St. Bernard*, the passage about his affection cannot be taken seriously ; he had been passionately devoted to Bernard for some years. The letter is evidently written for use or publication, and reveals a curious piece of acting.

Bernard's reply is also clearly 'part of the comedy,' as Hausrath says. Bernard is much addicted to *tutoyer* his friends, even his lady friends.[1] His previous letters to William, written before he was a ' son of religion ' and a devoted

[1] Witness his genial letter to our English Matilda.

follower, are written in that familiar style. But
in this brief note 'thou' and 'thine' become
'you' and 'your.' 'I consider your action both
just and necessary. The book itself, betraying
the mouth of those that speak iniquity, proves
that it was not idle. . . . But since I am not
accustomed, as you know well, to trust my own
judgment, especially in matters of such moment,'
it must wait a little. He will see William about
it after Easter. 'In the meantime be not impatient of my silence and forbearance in these
matters; most of them, indeed nearly all of them,
were not known to me before (cum horum
plurima et pene omnia hucusque nescierim).'

The letter is almost incomprehensible, coming
from such a man. *He* take the first discovery
of so influential a heretic so calmly; *he* not trust
his own judgment in such matters! Save for the
literary form, which is unmistakable, the letter
is wholly out of place in the bulky volume of
Bernard's correspondence. It is part of the play;
and its brevity and vagueness seem to indicate an
unwillingness or ethical discomfort on the part of
the writer.

The closing sentence in it has given trouble
even to Bernard's biographers, and must discon-

cert every admirer of the great uplifter of the twelfth century. Cotter Morison says ' he must refer to the special details' of Abélard's teaching. It is impossible to acquit the words of the charge of evasiveness and a half-conscious inaccuracy, even if they be so interpreted. We have already given the general considerations which compel us to think Bernard made himself fully acquainted with Abélard's opinions. We have already discussed the probability of his share in the driving of Abélard into Brittany. Other indications are not wanting. In 1132 Bernard was sent on a papal mission into Burgundy ; his companion was Joscelin, Abélard's early rival. Bernard attacks with some spirit the errors of an unnamed master in his *Treatise on Baptism* ; these errors are the opinions of Abélard. On one occasion, indeed, they had a direct controversy. Bernard had visited the Paraclete, and had criticised the way in which the nuns, following Abélard's direction, recited the Lord's Prayer. Abélard had inserted ' supersubstantial' for ' daily.' Heloise duly reported the criticism, and Abélard flew to arms. The letter was characteristic. A sweet and genial prelude, a crushing argumentative onslaught, and an ironical inversion of the charge. ' But let each do as he pleases,' the rhetorician concluded ; 'I do not wish to persuade any man to follow me in this. He may change the words of Christ as he likes.'

However, we need not strain detailed indications. It is impossible to think that Bernard was unacquainted with ' novelties' that the echo of a great name had borne to the ends of the earth.[1] When we have seen the whole story of Bernard's share in the struggle, it will be easier to understand this letter. It is puerile to think that we detract anything from the moral and spiritual greatness of St. Bernard in admitting an occasional approach to the common level of humanity. And there was present in strength that delusive ideal which has led so many good men into fields that were foreign to their native grandeur—the good of the Church.

There is no record of a conference with William of St. Thierry after Easter. The pupil has played his part, and he now vanishes completely from the theatre. But from the subsequent report which was sent to the pope, and

[1] *Fas est et ab hoste doceri.* The Benedictine defenders of Bernard (in *Migne*) say, in another connection : 'Was there a single cardinal or cleric in Rome who was unacquainted with his dogmas ?'

from the *Life of St. Bernard*, written by his admiring secretary, we learn that Bernard visited Abélard in private, and admonished him of his errors. The scene is unfortunately left to the imagination ; though the report we have mentioned speaks of a 'friendly and familiar admonition.' Bernard's biographer would have us believe that Abélard was quite subdued — the 'rhinoceros' was tamed again — by Bernard's brotherly address, and promised to retract his errors. It is possible that Abélard put him off with amiable generalities, but quite incredible that he made any such promise. We need not speculate, with Hausrath, on the probability of interference from his more ardent students. The episcopal report to the pope does not mention any broken promise. It could have used such a circumstance with great effect.

Then followed Bernard's second visit and warning. It would be difficult to say which dreaded the other more in these curious interviews, but Bernard had convinced himself of his duty to crush Abélard, and he was following out a very correct and excellently-devised scheme. The Gospel required a twofold personal correction of an erring brother, before he was denounced to the synagogue. The second one was to have witnesses. Bernard therefore boldly admonished Abélard in the presence of his students, and bade them burn the works of their master. It is a thousand pities we have no Abélardist record of these proceedings.

If Abélard said little during the conferences, he must have known that he was rapidly approaching another, perhaps a supreme, crisis in his life. He knew his Gospel, and he knew Bernard. The next step was the denunciation to the synagogue. He had had an experience of such denunciation, and he would certainly not expect a less insidious attack from the abbot of Clairvaux, who had avoided his dialectical skill so long. He determined to checkmate the Cistercians. Very shortly afterwards Bernard was dismayed to receive a letter from the Archbishop of Sens, in which he was invited to meet the redoubtable dialectician at Sens in a few weeks' time, and discuss the right and wrong of their quarrel before the whole spiritual and temporal nobility of France.

It was now a question of dialectics and rhetoric versus diplomacy ; though indeed we must credit Abélard—or his ' esquire,' as Bernard calls Arnold of Brescia—with a fine diplomatic move in claiming the discussion. There are several reasons for thinking that the Bishop of Paris was in Rome at the time, or the discussion should have been sought at Notre Dame. The next *instantia* was the Archbishop of Sens, and Abélard continued to assail that prelate until he was forced to accept the petition. Not improbably it appealed to the sporting instinct of old 'Henry the Boar,' a man of noble extraction, and of extremely worldly life before he fell under the influence of the ubiquitous Bernard. The quarrel of the two great luminaries of France was now notorious. He could not well refuse to open the lists for a superb trial by combat.

But Bernard had an entirely different theory of the condemnation of a heretic. He trusted to his personal influence and immense epistolary power. Abélard's works were available, and were sufficient for the grounding of a condemnation, he said. He was not merely impatient of the implied doubt of the infallibility of his judgment; he shrank nervously from the thought of such an encounter. He did not conceal for a moment his dread of Abélard's power. 'I am a boy beside him,' he pleaded, 'and he is a warrior from his youth.' On the other hand, if it became a question of a diplomatic struggle for a condemnation of the books at Rome, the positions would be exactly reversed. He refused to enter the lists with Abélard.

In the meantime the day which the Archbishop of Sens had appointed was rapidly approaching. It was the Octave of, or eighth day after, Pentecost. On the Sunday after Whitsunday, now dedicated to the Trinity, there was to be a brilliant religious function in the cathedral at Sens. It was customary to expose the relics to veneration on that day, and as Sens, the metropolitan church of Paris[1] and other important towns, had a very valuable collection of relics, the ceremony attracted a notable gathering of lords, spiritual and temporal. Louis VII. was to be there, with the usual escort of French nobles : the curiously compounded monarch had a profound veneration for relics, and something like a passion for the ceremonies that accompanied their translation, veneration, and so forth. All the suffragans of the archbishop would be present, with a number of other bishops, and abbots, clerics, and masters innumerable. Quite apart

---

[1] The see of Paris was not elevated into an archbishopric until a much later date.

from the duel between the greatest thinker and the greatest orator in Europe, there would be a very important and weighty gathering at the cathedral on that day. Abélard willingly assented. Bernard is fond of repeating in his later letters that Abélard set to work ' to summon his friends and followers from all parts.' We shall see that the only noteworthy supporters of Abélard at Sens were pupils or masters from Paris, which lay at a convenient distance. Bernard was shortly to lose his serenity in a sea of rhetoric.

There is a minor quarrel as to whether Bernard reversed his decision, and intimated his acceptance to the archbishop before the day arrived. Father Hefele thinks he did so. It is, however, clear that, in his letter to the pope afterwards, Bernard wishes to convey the impression that he held out until the last moment, and only yielded to the entreaties of his friends in actually presenting himself.

We shall refer to this letter to Pope Innocent shortly, but it is worth while to notice now the edifying picture he draws of his own preparation in contrast with that of ' the dragon.' Abélard is represented as feverishly whipping up his supporters, whilst Bernard refuses to hear of such

s

an encounter, not only on account of Abélard's
world-famed skill in debate, but also because he
thinks it improper to discuss sacred things in this
fashion. But friends represent that the Church
will suffer, and the enemies of Christ triumph.
Wearily and 'without preparation' — trusting
wholly in the divine promise of inspiration—he
presents himself on the appointed day before
'Goliath.'

In point of historical fact there is no reason
for thinking that Abélard made any effort to
gather supporters. The few we read of accompanied him from Paris. He had scarcely a single
friend in the ranks of his 'judges.' On the other
hand we *do* know that Bernard himself sent out
a strong and imperious 'whip' to his episcopal
supporters. There is a brief letter, contained in
the *Migne* collection, which was despatched to all
the French bishops on whom Bernard could rely
for sympathy and support. They have heard,
he says, of his summons to appear at Sens on
the Octave of Pentecost. 'If the cause were a
personal one,' he goes on, 'the child of your
holiness could perhaps not undeservedly look to
your support [patrocinium]. But it is your cause,
and more than yours; and so I admonish you

the more confidently and entreat you the more earnestly to prove yourselves friends in this necessity—friends, I should say, not of me, but of Christ.' And he goes on to prejudge the case in the mind of the official judges with his rhetorical denunciation of Abélard's heresies. 'Be not surprised,' he concludes, 'that I summon you so suddenly and with so brief a notice ; this is another ruse of our cunning adversary, so that he might meet us unprepared and unarmed.'

The consequence of the sending of this whip will be apparent when we come to examine the composition of the gathering at Sens. It marks the beginning of a period of most remarkable intrigue. The idyllic picture of the poor abbot making his way at the last moment to the assembly with a sublime trust in Providence and the righteousness of his cause must be regarded again at the close of the next chapter.

Whether Bernard formally accepted the summons or not, therefore, authentic information was conveyed to both sides that the debate would take place. It will be readily imagined how profoundly stirred the kingdom of France would be over such an expectation. The bare qualities of the antagonists put the discussion leagues above any remembered or contemporary event in the scholastic world ; the object of the debate—the validity of the new thought that was rapidly infecting the schools—was a matter of most material concern. Deutsch has a theory of the conflict which seems to be only notable as an illustration of the profundity of the Teutonic mind. He opines there may have been a political struggle underlying the academic demonstration. Louis was just beginning his struggle with Rome over the vexed question of investitures, and it is conceivable that the Abélardists leaned to the side of the king, in opposition to Bernard and the 'ultramontanes.' It is conceivable, but not at all probable. Abélard's sermon on St. Peter indicates a really ultramontane sentiment ; moreover, he has ever kept aloof from the political side of life. His follower, Arnold of Brescia, would be likely enough to fall in with any such regal design. Arnold was a young Luther, of premature birth. Born in Italy at the beginning of the twelfth century, he had travelled to France, and studied under Abélard, at an early age. He returned to Italy, and assumed the monastic habit. An enthusiastic idealist and a man of proportionate energy and audacity, he soon entered upon a fiery crusade against the sins of the monks, the clergy, and the hierarchy. He was driven from Italy in 1139, then from Switzerland, and he had just taken refuge in Paris when Bernard started his campaign. Since one of his most prominent theories was that the higher clergy should be stripped of all temporal privileges and possessions, his place is easily determined on the question of investitures. However, it is most unlikely that he should have dragged Abélard into these semi-political and dangerous questions. And although Bernard most sedulously urges the association of the hated Arnold with Abélard in his letters to Rome, he never mentions a suspicion of such a coalition as Deutsch suggests ; nor, in fine, does the conduct of the secular arm give the least countenance to the theory.

The conflict was inevitable, without the concurrence of any political intrigue. Abélard and Bernard were the natural representatives of schools which could no longer lie down in peace in the fold of the Church. Abélard foresaw disaster to the Church in the coming age of restless inquiry unless its truths could be formulated in his intellectual manner. Bernard was honestly convinced that Abélard was 'preparing the way for

Anti-Christ.' And it followed as a further consequence that Bernard should wish to avoid the discussion to which Abélard looked for salvation from the menace of the mystical school.

It will appear presently that Bernard was less concerned with the details of Abélard's teaching than with his spirit. He, however, dwells on them for controversial purposes, and they are certainly full of interest for the modern mind. The point will be more fully developed in a supplementary chapter. For the moment a brief glance at them will be instructive enough. They differ a little in Bernard's letter from the list given by William of St. Thierry, but one cannot even glance at them without noticing how remarkably this thinker of the twelfth century anticipated the judgment of the nineteenth century. His theses, like the theses of the advanced theology of these latter days, indicate two tendencies—an intellectual tendency to the more rational presentment of dogma, and an ethical tendency to the greater moralisation of ancient dogma.

We have already seen a good illustration of this anticipation of modern tendencies in Abélard's treatment of the traditional doctrines of heaven and hell respectively, and we shall see more later on. Of the fourteen specific points (thirteen in William's letter) contained in the present indictment, we may pass over most of those which refer to the Trinity as without interest. Abélard's phrases were new, but he cordially rejected the Arianism, Nestorianism, and so forth, with which Bernard insisted on crediting him. In the ninth proposition, that the species of bread and wine remain in the air after transubstantiation, and that adventurous mice only eat the species, not the Body of Christ, Abélard enunciated an opinion which has been widely adopted by modern Catholic theologians. In his second proposition, that the Holy Ghost was the Platonic *anima mundi*, Abélard was merely trying to save Plato from the damnation of the Bernardists.

On the ethical side, Abélard's theses (in their context in his works) are truly remarkable. Thus the third, 'That God can only do those things which He actually does, and in the way and at the time that He does them,' and the seventh, 'That God is not bound to prevent evil,' are obviously indications of an ethical attempt to save the sanctity of the Infinite in view of the triumph of evil. 'That Christ did not become Man for the purpose of saving us from the yoke of the devil' is an early formulation of the familiar modern conception of the Incarnation. 'That God does not do more for the elect, before they accept his grace, than for the damned,' and 'That we have shared the punishment but not the guilt of Adam,' are further clear anticipations of the refined theology of modern times. 'No man can sin before he exists,' said Abélard, to Bernard's mighty indignation. 'That God alone remits sin' is heretical to the modern Catholic, but the dogma was not completely born until the following century; [1] 'that evil thoughts, and even pleasure, are not of themselves sinful, but only the consent given to them,' and 'that the Jews who crucified Christ in ignorance did not sin, that acts which are done in ignorance cannot be sinful,' express the universal opinion of even modern Catholic theologians, in the sense in which Abélard held them.

And 'these,' wrote Bernard, with fine contempt, to his friend, Pope Innocent, 'are the chief errors of the theology, or rather the stultilogy, of Peter Abélard.'

[1] And the thesis is rejected in Abélard's *Apology*.

CHAPTER XIII

THE FINAL BLOW

On the 4th of June 1141, the cathedral at Sens was filled with one of the strangest throngs that ever gathered within its venerable walls. Church and state and the schools had brought their highest representatives and their motley thousands to witness the thrilling conflict of the two first thinkers and orators of France. On the previous day the magnificent ceremony of the veneration of the relics had taken place. At that ceremony the abbot of Clairvaux had discoursed of the meaning and potency of their act. And when the vast crowds of gentle and simple folk had quickened and sobbed and enthused at his burning words, he had ventured to ask their prayers for the conversion of an unbeliever, whom he did not name.

Now, on the Monday morning, the great concourse had streamed into the cathedral once

more, an intense eagerness flashing from the eyes
of the majority.   The red Mass of the Holy
Spirit had been chanted by the clerics, and the
clouds of incense still clung about the columns
and the vaulted roof of the church.   King Louis
sat expectant, and stupid, on the royal throne ;
the Count de Nevers and a brilliant group of
nobles and knights standing beside and behind
him.   Opposite them another gaily apparelled
group presented Henry, Archbishop of Sens,
with five of his suffragan bishops ; beside him
sat Samson, Archbishop of Rheims, with three
suffragans.   Mitred abbots added to the splen-
dour with their flash of jewels.   Shaven monks,
with the white wool of Cîteaux or the black tunic
of St. Benedict, mingled with the throng of
canons, clerics, scholastics, wandering masters,
ragged, cosmopolitan students, and citizens of
Sens and Paris in their gay holiday attire.

It was, at first sight, just such an assembly as
Abélard had dreamed of when he threw down the
gauntlet to the Cistercian.   But he must have
looked far from happy as he stood in the midst
of his small band of followers.   As he passed
into the cathedral, he had noticed Gilbert de la
Porée in the crowd, the brilliant master who was

to be Bernard's next victim, and he whispered
smilingly the line of Horace :

'It is thy affair when thy neighbour's house is on fire.'

With Abélard were the impetuous young master,
Bérenger of Poitiers ; the stern, ascetic, scornful
young Italian, Arnold of Brescia, flashing into
the eyes of the prelates the defiance that brought
him to the stake fourteen years afterwards ; and
the young Roman noble, Hyacinth, who afterwards became cardinal.

Beside these, and a host of admiring nonentities,
Abélard almost looked in vain for a friendly face
amidst the pressing throng. The truth was that,
as Rémusat says, 'if Bernard had not prepared
for debate, he had made every preparation for
the verdict.' The whole cathedral was with him.
After his discourse of the preceding day, and
the rumours that had preceded it, the priest-
ridden citizens of Sens were prepared to stone
the heretic, as the people of Soissons had
threatened to do. The students would be divided,
according to their schools. The monks longed
to see the downfall of their critic. The king—
the man who was to bear to his grave 'the curse
of Europe and the blessing of St. Bernard'—

was not likely to hesitate. The Count de Nevers was a pious, credulous noble, who afterwards became a Cistercian monk. Otto of Freising says Count Theobald of Champagne was present, though the report does not mention him ; in any case he had fallen largely under Bernard's influence since his sister had gone down in the *White Ship* in 1120. The clergy of Sens were with Bernard; their motto was : 'The church of Sens knows no novelties.' Of the judges proper, Geoffrey, Bishop of Chartres, was almost the only one who could be termed neutral ; and even he had now become greatly amenable to Bernard's influence. Archbishop Henry was completely in the hands of Bernard, his converter, who scolded him at times as if he were a boy. Archbishop Samson of Rheims owed his pallium to Bernard, in the teeth of the king's opposition ; he was deprived of it some years afterwards. Hugo of Mâcon, the aged Bishop of Auxerre, was a relative of Bernard's and a fellow-monk at Cîteaux. Joscelin of Vieri, Bishop of Soissons, was the former teacher of Goswin, and the associate of Bernard on a papal mission a few years before. Geoffrey, Bishop of Châlons, Abélard's former friend at St. Médard, had since been helped to a bishopric

by Bernard.   Hatto, Bishop of Troyes, had been
won to Bernard.   Alvise, Bishop of Arras, is said
to have been a brother of Abbot Suger and friend
of Goswin.   Of the only two other bishops
present, Helias of Orleans and Manasses of
Meaux, we have no information.

In such an assembly the nerve of the boldest
speaker might well fail.   Bernard had preached
during the Mass on the importance of the true
faith.   Then when the critical moment came, he
mounted the pulpit with a copy of the writings
of Abélard, and the dense crowd, totally ignorant,
most probably, of previous events, which were
known only to the intimate friends of each com-
batant, held its breath for the opening of the
struggle.   The frail, worn, nervous figure in the
flowing, white tunic began to read the indictment,
but suddenly Abélard stepped forth before the
astonished judges, and, crying out : 'I will not
be judged thus like a criminal ; I appeal to Rome,'
turned his back on them and strode out of the
cathedral.

Chroniclers have left to our imagination the
confusion that followed, and we may leave it to
that of the reader.   Although the bishops afterwards made a show of disputing it, the appeal

was quite canonical, and was admitted at Rome. But it was a course which had not entered into the thoughts of the most astute of them, and which completely upset their plans. They could not now touch the person of Abélard. Bernard, indeed, did not deprive the great audience of the discourse he had 'not prepared,' although it was now quite safe from contradiction. We have it, some say, in his later letter to the pope, a most vehement denunciation and often perversion of Abélard's teaching. He gained an easy victory, as far as Sens was concerned. The next day the prelates met together, condemned Abélard's teaching as heretical, and forwarded a report, submitting his person and his works, to Rome.

The question why Abélard behaved in so extraordinary a manner has had many answers. The answer of the godly, given by Bernard's monkish biographer, is of the transcendental order. Brother Geoffrey relates that Abélard confessed to his intimate friends that he mysteriously lost the use and control of his mind when Bernard began. Bishop Otto of Freising says that he feared 'a rising of the people.' He would be more likely to provoke one by thus affronting their great cathedral and prelates. The true interpretation is that the assembly was a play, covering an unworthy in-trigue, and he had been secretly informed of it. The bishops had drawn up their verdict, over their cups, on the preceding day.

Desperate efforts are made, of course, to destroy an interpretation which does not leave the dis-credit on Abélard, but it has now been based on incontrovertible evidence. In the first place the bishops ingenuously confess it themselves in their eagerness to evade a different accusation. In order to influence the judgment, or rather the decision, of the pope, they told him that they had found Abélard's teaching to be heretical. How, then, were they to reconcile this with the notice of Abélard's appeal to Rome? 'We had,' they say in their report, 'already condemned him on the day before he appealed to you.' It matters little who wrote this report—whether Bernard [1] or Henry's secretary—because it was signed by the bishops. They reveal their secret conclave of the Sunday evening. Henry was particularly anxious to justify them, at all costs, on the charge of

[1] It is singular that Mr. Poole, who credits Bernard with writing the report, should speak of the words as a deliberate 'lie of excuse,' especially as he adopts the witness of Bérenger to a previous con-demnation. We are not only compelled by independent evidence to take them as correct, but one imputes a lesser sin to Bernard (from the Catholic point of view) in doing so.

disregarding the appeal, because he had been suspended by Innocent for that offence a few years previously.

Again, in the *Historia Pontificalis*, attributed to John of Salisbury, there is an account of Bernard's attempt to secure the condemnation of that other brilliant dialectician, Gilbert de la Porée, in 1148. It is expressly stated that Bernard called the chief personages together the night before the synod, and was leading them to pronounce on Gilbert's 'errors,' when an archdeacon of Châlons spoiled his strategy. Further, the writer goes on to say that the cardinals—there were a number present for the synod—were greatly incensed with Bernard, and 'said that Abbot Bernard had beaten Master Abélard by a similar stratagem.' It is not unlikely that they learned the story from Hyacinth, the young Roman.

The classical witness to this over-night conclave is Abélard's pupil, Bérenger of Poitiers. Unfortunately, his narrative is marred by obvious exaggerations and a careless, heated temper. It occurs in an apology for Abélard, or an 'open letter' to Bernard, which he wrote some months afterwards. After reminding Bernard of some of the frivolities of his early youth, and much sarcastic comment on his actual reputation, he gives what purports to be a detailed description of the secret meeting. No one who reads it will take it literally. Yet when, in later years, he was run down, like Gilbert and Arnold, by the relentless sleuthhound, he made a partial retractation. What he has written as to the person of 'the man of God' must, he says, be taken as a joke. But a few lines previously he has appealed to this very narrative in justification of his abuse of Bernard : 'Let the learned read my "Apology," and they may justly censure me if I have unduly blamed him [Bernard].' It is not impossible that Bérenger merely retracts such remarks as that about Bernard's juvenile 'cantiunculas.' In any case, we may justly transcribe a portion of the narrative, after these qualifications.

'At length, when the dinner was over, Peter's work was brought in, and some one was directed to read it aloud. This fellow, animated with a hatred of Peter, and well watered with the juice of the grape, read in a much louder voice than he had been asked to do. After a time you would have seen them knock their feet together, laugh, and crack jokes ; you would think they were honouring Bacchus rather than Christ. And all the time the cups are going, the wine is being praised, the episcopal throats are being moistened. The juice of the lethal drink had already buried their hearts. . . . Then, when anything unusually subtle and divine was read out, anything the episcopal ears were not accustomed to, they hardened their hearts and ground their teeth against Peter. "Shall we let this monster live?" they cried. . . . The heat of the wine at length relaxed the eyes of all in slumber. The reader continues amidst their snoring. One leans on his elbow in order to sleep. Another gets a soft cushion. Another slumbers with his head resting on his knees. So when the reader came to anything particularly thorny in Peter, he shouted in the deaf ears of the pontiffs: "Do you condemn?" And some of them just waking up at the last syllable, would mutter: "We condemn."'

It is not difficult to take off the due and considerable discount from the youthful extravagance of Master Bérenger. Bernard's followers (in the *Histoire littéraire de la France*) say he had 'too noble a soul and too elevated a sentiment to stoop to the refutation of such a work.' He has never, at all events, essayed to rebut the charge of procuring a verdict against Abélard on the day before the synod. Even in our own days it is a familiar source of merriment in ecclesiastical and monastic circles to see a group of prelates fervently following the red Mass of the Holy Ghost as a preliminary to a discussion of points which they have notoriously settled over their cups the night before. Such a meeting of the bishops on the Sunday would be inevitable. Bernard would inevitably be present, and Abélard infallibly excluded. In any case, the evidence is too precise and substantial to be rejected. Indeed, the story fully harmonises with our knowledge of Bernard's earlier and subsequent conduct. It is not ours to inquire minutely how far Bernard was consistent with himself and his lofty ideals in acting thus.

Bernard was defeated for the moment by the unexpected appeal from the verdict of the unjust judges. But he knew well that Abélard had avoided Scylla only to plunge into Charybdis. Abélard's knowledge of the curia was restricted to a few days' acquaintance with it in a holiday mood at Morigni. Arnold of Brescia probably urged his own acquaintance with it in vain. Moreover many years had elapsed since his name was inscribed by the side of that of Bernard in the chronicle of Morigni. Bernard, the secluded contemplative, knew the curia well. He hastened home, told his secretary to prepare for a journey across the Alps, and sat down to write a batch of extremely clever epistles. The battle was fought and won before Abélard had covered many leagues in the direction of Italy.

The first document that Bernard seems to have written is the report upon the synod which was sent to Innocent ii. in the name of the Archbishop of Rheims and his suffragans. Hausrath, who is the least restrained by considerations of Bernard's official sanctity of all Abélard's apologists, and others, hold that both the reports of the proceedings, that of Samson and that of Henry (for the two archbishops, with their respective suffragans, reported separately to the pope), were written by Bernard. It is at least clear that the Rheims report was drawn up by him. Mr. Poole says this is admitted even by Father Hefele. Bernard's style is indeed unmistakable.

In this official document, therefore, the pope is informed, not so much that a dispute about Abélard's orthodoxy is referred to his court, as that 'Peter Abélard is endeavouring to destroy the merit of faith, in that he professes himself able to comprehend by his human reason the whole being of God.' From this gross calumny[1] the writer passes on to assure the pope that Abélard 'is a great man in his own eyes, ever disputing about the faith to its undoing, walking in things that are far above him, a searcher into the divine majesty, a framer of heresies.' He goes on to recount that Abélard's book had been condemned and burnt once before, at Soissons, 'because of the iniquity that was found in it'; whereas every scholar in France knew that it was condemned on the sole ground that it had been issued without authorisation. 'Cursed be he who has rebuilt the walls of Jericho,' fulminates the abbot of Clairvaux. Finally, he represents Abélard as boasting of his influence at Rome. 'This is the boast of the man,' he says, 'that his book can find wherein to rest its head in the Roman curia. This gives strength and assurance to his frenzy.' The sole object of his appeal is 'to secure a longer immunity for his iniquity. You must needs apply a swift remedy to this source of contagion.' And the monstrous epistle closes with a trust that Innocent will do his part, and that swiftly, as they had done theirs.

---

[1] Abélard explicitly and very emphatically rebukes such pretension in the very books which Bernard is supposed to have read.

Thus was the pope introduced, in a handwriting he had so many reasons to respect, to Abélard's appeal for consideration.

The second report, which is signed by Archbishop Henry and his suffragans, and which may not have been drawn up by Bernard, is more free from diplomatic turnings, but also gravely unjust to the appellant. It gives the pope a lengthy account of the order of events since the receipt of the letter of William of St. Thierry. From it we have quoted the words in which the bishops themselves confess the secret conclave on the Sunday. The bishops were affronted, it says, by Abélard's appeal, which was 'hardly canonical,' but they were content with an examination of his doctrines (consisting of Bernard's vehement harangue) and found them to be 'most manifestly heretical.' They therefore 'unanimously demand the condemnation of Abélard.' To put the point quite explicitly, the pope is clearly to understand that the Church of France has already dealt with Abélard. It is not quite so insidious as the report which Bernard wrote, and to which—sad sign of the growing quality of the Church—even Geoffrey of Chartres lent his venerable name.

Bernard's official task seemed to be at an end

with the despatch of the report. His profound
and generous trust in the Holy Spirit would lead
one to expect a complete withdrawal from the
quarrel into which he had been so unwillingly
forced. But Bernard's conception of the activity
of the Holy Spirit, though equal in theoretical
altitude, was very different in practice from that
of a Francis of Assisi. We have amongst his
works no less than three epistles that he wrote at
the time to Pope Innocent in his own name. One
of them consists of a few prefatory remarks to
the list of Abélard's errors. The two others are
of a much more personal and interesting character.
It is difficult to say whether, and if so, why, the
two letters were sent to the pope, but it is not
necessary to determine this. Both were certainly
written by Bernard for the purpose.

The first letter is addressed ' to his most loving
father and lord, Innocent, Sovereign Pontiff by
the grace of God, from Brother Bernard, called
the abbot of Clairvaux.' From the first line he
aims at determining the case in the pope's mind.
' It is necessary that there be scandals amongst us
—necessary, but assuredly not welcome.' Hence
have the saints ever longed to be taken from this
troubled world. Bernard is equally tired of life.

He knows not whether it be expedient that he die, yet 'the scandals and troubles' about him are pressing his departure. 'Fool that I was to promise myself rest if ever the Leonine trouble [1] was quelled and peace was restored to the Church. That trouble is over, yet I have not found peace. I had forgotten that I still lingered in the vale of tears.' His sorrow and his tears have been renewed. 'We have escaped the lion [Pierleone], only to meet the dragon [Abélard], who, in his insidious way, is perhaps not less dangerous than the lion roaring in high places. Did I say insidious ? Would indeed that his poisoned pages did lurk in the library, and were not read openly in the streets. His books fly in all directions ; whereas they, in their iniquity, once shunned the light, they now emerge into it, thinking the light to be darkness. . . . A new gospel is being made for the nations, a new faith is put before them.' After Pierleone it is useful to remind Innocent of his second great *bête noire*. 'The Goliath [Abélard] stalks along in his greatness, girt about with that noble panoply of his, and preceded by his weapon-bearer, Arnold of Brescia. Scale is

[1] The reference is to the anti-pope, a Pierleone. It is a subtle reminder of what Pope Innocent owes to Bernard.

joined to scale, so closely that not a breath can get between.[1]   For the French bee [Abeille-ard] has hummed its call to the Italian bee ; and they have conspired together against the Lord and his anointed.'   He must even deny them the merit of their notoriously ascetic lives : ' Bearing the semblance of piety in their food and clothing, but void of its virtue, they deceive many by transforming themselves into angels of light—whereas they are devils.'   The pope must not be misled by rumours of Abélard's present fervour of life ; he is ' outwardly a Baptist, but inwardly a Herod,' Bernard assures him.   Then follows a passage we have already quoted.   He tells the pope the edifying story of the archbishop's summons, his refusal, the entreaties of his friends, the gathering of Abélard's supporters, and his final resolve to go : ' Yielding to the counsel of my friends, I presented myself at the appointed time and place, unprepared and unequipped, save that I had in mind the monition : " Take ye no thought what and how ye shall speak." '   Then ' when his books had begun to be read [he does not say by whom], he would not listen, but went out, appealing from the judges he had chosen.   These things I tell

---

[1] Recalling some of the zoology of the Old Testament.

thee in my own defence, lest thou mayst think I
have been too impetuous or bold in the matter.
But thou, O successor of Peter, thou shalt decide
whether he who has assailed the faith of Peter
should find refuge in the see of Peter.' In other
words, do not allow Abélard to come to Rome,
but condemn him unheard, on my word. He
ends with a final diplomatic *argumentum ad in-
vidiam*. 'Hyacinth has done me much injury,
but I have thought well to suffer it, seeing that he
did not spare you and your court when he was at
Rome, as my friend, and indeed yours, Nicholas,
will explain more fully by word of mouth.'

The second letter runs so largely on the same
lines that it is thought by some to have been sent
to the pope instead of the preceding, in which the
reference to Hyacinth and the curia may have
been impolitic. 'Weeping has the spouse of
Christ wept in the night,' it begins, 'and tears are
upon her cheeks; there is none to console her
out of all her friends. And in the delaying of the
spouse, to thee, my lord, is committed the care of
the Shunammite in this land of her pilgrimage.'
Abélard is a 'domestic enemy,' an Absalom, a
Judas. There is the same play upon the lion and
the dragon, and upon the scaly monster formed

of Abélard and Arnold. 'They have become corrupt and abominable in their aims, and from the ferment of their corruptions they pervert the faith of the simple, disturb the order of morals, and defile the chastity of the Church.' Moreover Abélard 'boasts that he has opened the founts of knowledge to the cardinals and priests of the Roman curia, and that he has lodged his books and his opinions in the hands and hearts of the Romans ; and he adduces as patrons of his error those who should judge and condemn him.' He concludes with an apostrophe to Abélard, which was well calculated to expel the last lingering doubt from the mind of the pope. 'With what thoughts, what conscience, canst thou have recourse to the defender of the faith—thou, its persecutor ? With what eyes, what brow, wilt thou meet the gaze of the friend of the Spouse — thou, the violator of His bride ? Oh, if the care of the brethren did not detain me ! If bodily infirmity did not prevent it ! How I should love to see the friend of the Spouse defending the bride in His absence !'

The third letter, a kind of preface to Bernard's list of errors and commentary thereon, is of the same unworthy temper, tortuous, diplomatic,

misleading, and vituperative. It is not apparent
on what ground Hausrath says this commentary
represents Bernard's speech at Sens ; if it does so,
we have another curious commentary on Bernard's
affirmation that he went to the synod unprepared.
However that may be, the letter is a singular
composition, when we remember that it accompanied an appeal to a higher court, to which the
case had been reserved. It opens with a declaration that 'the see of Peter' is the due and natural
tribunal to which to refer 'all scandals that arise
in the Kingdom of God'; a declaration which is
hardly consistent with the assurance, when it is
necessary to defend their condemnation of Abélard,
that his appeal 'seems to us wonderful.' Then
follows the familiar caricature. 'We have here in
France an old master who has just turned theologian, who has played with the art of rhetoric from
his earliest years and now raves about the Holy
Scriptures [Abélard had been teaching Scripture
and theology for the last twenty-six years]. He
is endeavouring to resuscitate doctrines that were
condemned and buried long ago, and to these he
adds new errors of his own. A man who, in his
inquiries into all there is in heaven above or earth
below, is ignorant of nothing save the word "I do

not know." He lifts his eyes to the heavens, and peers into the hidden things of God, then returns to us with discourse of things that man is not permitted to discuss.' This last sentence, considered as a charge by Bernard of Clairvaux against others, is amusing. Bernard spent half his time in searching the hidden things of God, and the other half in discoursing of them. But Abélard conceived them otherwise than he.

Thus was the supreme judge instructed in his part, whilst the foolish Abélard lingered idly in Paris, not improbably, as Bernard says, boasting of his friends at the curia. It was very possible that he had friends at Rome. Deutsch suspects the existence of a faction in the sacred college, which was opposed to Innocent and the Chancellor Haymerick, and would be favourable to Abélard. Bernard was not the man to leave a single risk unchallenged—or to the care of the Holy Ghost.

In the first place, therefore, he wrote a circular letter ' to all my lords and fathers, the venerable bishops and cardinals of the curia, from the child of their holiness.' His secretary was to deliver a copy to each. 'None will doubt,' he says, ' that it is your especial duty to remove all scandals from the kingdom of God.' The Roman

Church is the tribunal of the world : 'to it we do well to refer, not questions, but attacks on the faith and dishonour of Christ : contumely and contempt of the fathers : present scandals and future dangers. The faith of the simple is derided, the hidden things of God are dragged forth, questions of the most sublime mysteries are rashly debated, insults are offered to the fathers.' They will see this by the report. 'And if you think there is just ground for my agitation, be ye also moved'—and moved to take action. 'Let him who has raised himself to the heavens be crushed down to hell ; he has sinned in public, let him be punished in public.' It is the fulmination of the prophet of the age on the duty of the curia.

Then came eight private letters to cardinals of his acquaintance, an interesting study in ecclesiastical diplomacy. To the chancellor of the curia, Haymerick, he speaks chiefly of Abélard's boast of friends at court. He transcribes the passage from his letter to Innocent ; and he adds the earlier allusion to the Roman deacon, Hya-cinth, who was evidently a thorn in the side of the officials of the curia. To Guido of Castello, afterwards Celestine II., who was known to be a friend of Abélard, he writes in an entirely new strain. 'I should do you wrong,' he begins, 'if I thought you so loved any man as to embrace his errors also in your affection.' Such a love would be animal, earthly, diabolical. Others may say what they like of Guido, but Bernard is a man who 'never judges anybody without proof,' and he will not believe it. He passes to a mild complaint that 'Master Peter introduces profane novelties in his books'; still 'it is not I that accuse him before the Father, but his own book.' But he cannot refrain from putting just a little *venenum in cauda* : 'It is expedient for you and for the Church that silence be imposed on him whose mouth is full of curses and bitterness and guile.'

Cardinal Ivo, on the other hand, belongs to the loyal group. 'Master Peter Abélard,' he is told, 'a prelate without dependency, observes no order and is restrained by no order. . . . He is a Herod in his soul, a Baptist in outward appearance.' However, that is not my business, says the diplomatist, 'every man shall bear his own burden.' Bernard is concerned about his heresies, and his boast that he will be protected by a certain faction in the curia. Ivo must do his duty 'in

freeing the Church from the lips of the wicked.'
A young unnamed cardinal is appealed to for
support. 'Let no man despise thy youth,'
begins the man who calls Abélard a 'slippery
serpent'; 'not grey hair but a sober mind is
what God looks to.' Another cardinal, who had
a custom of rising when any person entered his
room, is playfully approached with a reminder of
this : 'If thou art indeed a son of the Church,'
the note ends, 'defend the womb that has borne
thee and the breasts that have suckled thee.'
Guido of Pisa receives a similar appeal : 'If thou
art a son of the Church, if thou knowest the
breast of thy mother, desert her not in her peril.'
The letter to another Cardinal Guido is particularly
vicious and unworthy. 'I cannot but write you,'
it begins, 'of the dishonour to Christ, the trials
and sorrows of the Church, the misery of the
helpless, and groans of the poor.' What is the
matter ? This : 'We have here in France a monk
who observes no rule, a prelate without care,
an abbot without discipline, one Peter Abélard,
who disputes with boys and busies himself with
women.' There is a nasty ambiguity in the last
phrase. Again, 'We have escaped the roar of the
lion [Pierleone] only to hear the hissing of the

dragon Peter. . . . If the mouth of the wicked be not closed, may He who alone regards our works consider and condemn.' A similar letter is addressed to Cardinal Stephen of Praeneste. 'I freely write to you, whom I know to be a friend of the spouse, of the trials and sorrows of the spouse of Christ.' Abélard is 'an enemy of Christ,' as is proved, not only by his works, but by 'his life and actions.' He has 'sallied forth from his den like a slippery serpent'; he is 'a hydra,' growing seven new heads where one has been cut off. He 'misleads the simple,' and finally 'boasts that he has inoculated the Roman curia with the poison of his novelty.'

A ninth letter is addressed to an abbot who was in Rome at the time, and who is drawn into the intrigue with many holy threats. 'If any man is for the Lord let him take his place. The truth is in danger. Peter Abélard has gone forth to prepare the way for Anti-Christ. . . . .May God consider and condemn, if the mouth of the wicked be not closed forthwith.'

These letters were handed over, for personal delivery, to Bernard's monk-secretary, Nicholas; in many of them it is expressly stated that the bearer will enlarge upon the text more freely by word of mouth. We know enough about this monk to be assured of the more than fidelity with which he accomplished his task. Enjoying the full confidence of Bernard at that time, a very able and well-informed monk, Nicholas de Montier-Ramey was a thorough scoundrel, as Bernard learned to his cost a few years afterwards. He had to be convicted of forging Bernard's seal and hand for felonious purposes before the keen scent of the abbot discovered his utter unscrupulousness.

With Abélard lingering at Paris in his light-hearted way, the violence and energy of Bernard swept away whatever support he might have counted on at Rome. Throughout the curia Bernard had scattered his caricature of Abélard : a lawless monk, an abbot who neglected his abbey, a man of immoral life, an associate of the recognised enemies of the papacy, already condemned for heresy, a reviver of Arius and Nestorius and Pelagius, a teacher without reverence, a disturber of the faith of the simple. The pope did not hesitate a moment ; the letters sent to him are masterpieces of diplomatic correspondence. The waverers in the curia were most skilfully worked. In mere secular matters such an attempt to corrupt the judges would be fiercely resented. Bernard lived in a transcendental region, that Hegelian land in which contradictions disappear.

It was on the 4th of June that Abélard appealed to Rome. There were no Alpine tunnels in those days, and the journey from Paris to Rome was a most formidable one. Yet Bernard's nervous energy had infused such spirit into the work, and he had chosen so able a messenger, that the whole case was ended in less than seven weeks. There cannot have been a moment's hesitation at Rome. On the 16th of July the faithful of Rome gathered about the door of St. Peter's for the solemn reading of the decree of excommunication. The pope was there, surrounded by his cardinals, and it was announced, with the usual impressive flourishes, that Abélard's works were condemned to the flames and his person to be imprisoned by the ecclesiastical authorities. Rome has not been a model of the humane use of power, but she has rarely condemned a man unheard. On the sole authority of Bernard the decree recognised in Abélard's 'pernicious doctrine' the already condemned errors of the early heresiarchs. Arnold of Brescia, who had not been officially indicted, was included in the condemnation. It was

Bernard's skilful use of his association with Abélard which chiefly impelled the pope. Innocent replies to Bernard's appeal by sending back to him the decree of the condemnation of his antagonist, with a private note to the effect that it must not be published until after it has been read at an approaching synod.

CHAPTER XIV

CONSUMMATUM EST

It was well for Bernard's cause that he succeeded in obtaining the decree without delay. He had carefully represented that the whole of France supported him in his demand. It does seem as if some of Abélard's friends were puzzled for a time by his appeal, but before long there came a reaction in his favour, just as had happened after his condemnation at Soissons. Bernard himself may have been perfectly self-justified in his determined effort to prevent Abélard from having a fair chance of defending himself, but there are two ways of regarding his conduct.[1] Abélard's followers naturally adopted the view

[1] I abstain from commenting on St. Bernard's conduct, or making the ethical and psychological analysis of it, which is so imperfectly done by his biographers at this period, because they do not fully state the facts, or not in their natural order. It would be a fascinating task, but one beside the purpose of the present work and not discreet for the present writer. I have let Bernard speak for himself.

which was less flattering to Bernard's reputation, and they seem to have had some success in enforcing it. In a letter of Bernard's to a certain cardinal we find him defending himself against the charge of 'having obtained the decree by improper means [*subripere*] from the pope.'

One of the chief instruments in the agitation on the Abélardist side was the apology of Bérenger of Poitiers, which we have quoted previously. Violent and coarse as it was, it was known to have a foundation of fact ; and, in the growing unpopularity of Bernard, it had a wide circulation. It was not answered, as the Benedictines say ; yet we may gather from Bérenger's qualified withdrawal of it, when he is hard pressed, that it gave Bernard and the Cistercians a good deal of annoyance. Arnold of Brescia was, meanwhile, repeating his fulminations at Paris against the whole hierarchical system. He had taken Abélard's late chair in the chapel of St. Hilary on the slope of St. Genevieve, and was sustaining the school until the master should return from Rome in triumph. But Arnold had no hope of any good being done at Rome, and rather preached rebellion against the whole of the bejewelled prelates. Sternly ascetic in his life and ideals—St. Bernard scoffingly

applies to him the evangelical description of the
Baptist : ' He ate not, neither did he drink '—
he was ever contrasting the luxurious life of the
pastors of the Church with the simple ideal of
early Christianity.   He had not such success in
France as elsewhere, and Bernard secured his
expulsion a few years later.   But the same stern
denunciation was on his noble lips when the savage
flames sealed them for ever, under the shadow of
St. Peter's, in 1155.

Abélard himself seems to have taken matters
with a fatal coolness, whilst his adversary was
moving heaven and earth to destroy him.   He
allowed a month or two to elapse before he
turned in the direction of Rome.[1]   Secure in the
consciousness of the integrity of his cause and
his own power of pleading, and presuming too
much of Rome's proud boast that it ' condemned
no man unheard,' he saw no occasion for hurry.
Late in the summer he set out upon his long
journey.   It was his purpose to travel through
Burgundy and Lyons, and to cross the Alps by
the pass which was soon to bear the name of
his energetic enemy.   After the fashion of all

[1] He did, however, write an ' apology ' or defence, but only a few
fragments of it survive.

travellers of the time he rested at night in the monastery nearest to the spot where he was overtaken. Thus it came to pass that, when he arrived in the neighbourhood of Mâcon, he sought hospitality of the great and venerable Benedictine abbey at Cluny.

Peter the Venerable, abbot of Cluny, was the second monk in France at that time. A few degrees lower in the scale of neural intensity than his canonised rival, he far surpassed him in the less exalted virtues of kindliness, humanity, and moderation. 'The rule of St. Benedict,' he once wrote to Bernard, 'is dependent on the sublime general law of charity'; that was not the route to the honour of canonisation. He belonged by birth to the illustrious family of the Montboissiers of Auvergne, and was a man of culture, fine and equable temper, high principle, gentle and humane feeling, and much practical wisdom. He had had more than one controversy with the abbot of Clairvaux, and his influence was understood to counterbalance that of Bernard at times in the affairs of the Church and the kingdom.

It was, therefore, one of the few fortunate accidents of his career that brought Abélard to Cluny at that time. Abbot Peter knew that

Bernard had actually in his possession the papal
decree which ordered the imprisonment of Abélard
and the burning of his books. He had a deep
sympathy for the ageing master who was seeking
a new triumph in Rome under such peculiarly
sad circumstances. Peter knew well how little
the question of heresy really counted for in the
matter. It was a question of Church politics;
and he decided to use his influence for the
purpose of securing a tranquil close for the
embittered and calumniated life. Abélard was
beginning to feel the exactions of his journey,
and remained some days at the abbey. The
abbot, as he afterwards informs the pope, spoke
with him about his purpose, and at length informed him that the blow had already fallen. It
was the last and decisive blow. The proud head
never again raised itself in defiance of the potent
ignorance, the crafty passion, and the hypocrisy
that made up the world about him. He was too
much enfeebled, too much dispirited, even to
repeat the blasphemy of his earlier experience:
'Good Jesus, where art thou?' For the first
and last time he bowed to the mystery of the
triumph of evil.

Abbot Peter then undertook the task of avert-

ing the consequence of Bernard's triumph, and
found little difficulty in directing the fallen man.
It was imperative, in the first place, to effect
some form of reconciliation between the great
antagonists, so as to disarm the hostility of
Bernard.   We shortly find Raynard, the abbot
of Cîteaux, at Cluny, and Abélard accompanies
him back to his abbey.   Peter has obtained from
him a formal promise to correct anything in his
works that may be 'offensive to pious ears,' and
on this basis Bernard is invited to a reconciliation
at Cîteaux.   A few days afterwards Abélard returns to Cluny with the laconic reply that they
'had had a peaceful encounter,' as the abbot
informs the pope, to whom he immediately writes
for permission to receive Abélard into their community at Cluny, adding, with a calm contempt
of the accusation of heresy, that 'Brother Peter's
knowledge' will be useful to the brethren.   The
abbot of Cluny had claims upon the pope's consideration.   Although the anti-pope, Anacletus,
had been a monk of Cluny, Peter had been the
first to meet Innocent when he came to France
for support.   In pointed terms he begged that
Abélard 'might not be driven away or troubled
by the importunity of any persons.'   His request

was granted ; and thus the broken spirit was spared that 'public humiliation' in France that Bernard had demanded.

The basis of reconciliation with Bernard was probably a second and shorter apology which Abélard wrote at Cluny. It was convenient to regard this at the time as a retractation. In reality it is for the most part a sharp rejection of Bernard's formulation of his theses and a new enunciation of them in more orthodox phraseology. His frame of mind appears in the introductory note.

'There is a familiar proverb that "Nothing is said so well that it cannot be perverted," and, as St. Jerome says, "He who writes many books invites many judges." I also have written a few things—though little in comparison with others—and have not succeeded in escaping censure ; albeit in those things for which I am so gravely charged I am conscious of no fault, nor should I obstinately defend it, if I were. It may be that I have erred in my writings, but I call God to witness and to judge in my soul that I have written nothing through wickedness or pride of those things for which I am chiefly blamed.'

Then, warmly denying Bernard's charge that

he has ever taught a secret doctrine, he passes to a detailed profession of faith on the lines of Bernard's list of errors. With regard to the Trinity he denies all the heresies ascribed to him ; this he could do with perfect justice. On the other points he makes distinctions, adds explanations and qualifications, and even sometimes accepts Bernard's thesis without remark, though one can generally see a reserve in the background. Thus, on the question of sin committed in ignorance, he makes the familiar modern distinction between culpable and inculpable ignorance : he admits that we have inherited Adam's sin, but adds 'because his sin is the source and cause of all our sins.' On the question of the prevention of evil by God, he merely says, 'Yes, He often does'; and so forth. The only sentence which looks like a real retractation is that in which he grants 'the power of the keys' to all the clergy. In this he clearly dissociates himself from Arnold of Brescia, and perplexes his friends. But his earlier teaching on the point is by no means so clear and categorical as that of Arnold. There is nothing either very commendable or very condemnable about the document. It probably represents a grudging concession to the abbot of Cluny's friendly pressure and counsel to withdraw from what was really only a heated quarrel with as little friction as possible. That Abélard was not in the penitent mood some writers discover in the letter is clear from the peroration. 'My friend [!] has concluded his list of errors with the remark : "They are found partly in Master Peter's book of theology, partly in his *Sentences*, and partly in his *Scito te Ipsum*." But I have never written a book of *Sentences*, and therefore the remark is due to the same malice or ignorance as the errors themselves.'

However, the document had a sufficient air of retractation about it to allow Bernard to withdraw. In substance and spirit it was, as its name indicated, an apology, not a retractation. In fact Bernard's zealous secretary and an unknown abbot attacked the apology, but Abélard made no reply, and the discussion slowly died away. Bernard had won a political triumph, and he showed a becoming willingness to rest content with empty assurances. Abélard's personal force was dead ; little eagerness was shown to pursue the seminal truths he had left behind, and which were once thought so abhorrent and pernicious. Later Benedictines virtually admit the justice of this.

Mabillon says : 'We do not regard Abélard as
a heretic ; it is sufficient for the defence of
Bernard to admit that he erred in certain things.'
And the historian Noël Alexandre also says, ' He
must not be regarded as a heretic.' Indeed,
Bernard was strongly condemned at the time by
English and German writers. Otto of Freising
reproves his action in the cases of both Abélard
and Gilbert, and attributes it to defects of character. John of Salisbury severely criticises him
in the *Historia Pontificalis* ; and Walter Map,
another English writer, voices the same widespread
feeling.

Another document that Abélard sent out from
Cluny forms the last page of his intercourse with
Heloise. If he had wearily turned away from
the strange drama of life, his affection for her
survives the disillusion in all its force. There is
a welcome tenderness in his thought of her amidst
the crushing desolation that has fallen upon him.
She shall not be hurt by any unwilling impression
of persistent calumny. He writes to her a most
affectionate letter, and in the sanctuary of their
love makes a solemn profession of the purity of
his faith.

' My sister Heloise, once dear to me in the

world, and now most dear in Christ, logic has brought the enmity of men upon me. For there are certain perverse calumniators, whose wisdom leads to perdition, that say I take pre-eminence in logic but fail egregiously in the interpretation of Paul; commending my ability, they would deny me the purity of Christian faith . . . I would not rank as a philosopher if it implied any error in faith; I would not be an Aristotle if it kept me away from Christ. For no other name is given to me under heaven in which I may find salvation. I adore Christ, sitting at the right hand of the Father.' Then follows a brief confession of faith on the chief points of Christian belief—the Trinity, the Incarnation, baptism, penance, and the resurrection. 'And that all anxiety and doubt may be excluded from thy heart,' he concludes, 'do thou hold this concerning me, I have grounded my conscience on that rock on which Christ has built His Church.'

It was Abélard's farewell to her who had shared so much of the joy and the bitterness of his life. But what a different man it recalls through the mists of time from the 'dragon' of Bernard's letters! One contrast at least we cannot fail to note between the saint and the sinner. We have seen Bernard's treatment of Abélard ; in this private letter, evidently intended for no eye but that of his wife, we have the sole recorded utterance of Abélard on the man who, for so little reason, shattered the triumph and the peace of his closing years.

For if there is a seeming peace about the few months of life that still remained to the great teacher, it is the peace of the grave—the heavy peace that shrouds a dead ambition and a broken spirit, not the glad peace that adorns requited labour and successful love. Abélard enters upon a third stage of his existence, and the shadow of the tomb is on it. He becomes a monk ; he centres all his thought on the religious exercises that, like the turns of the prayer wheel, write the long catalogue of merit in heaven.

In the abbey of Cluny, under the administration of Peter the Venerable, he found all that his soul desired in its final stage. The vast monastery had a community of four hundred and sixty monks. Older than its rival, Cîteaux, possessed of great wealth and one of the finest churches in France, it was eagerly sought by monastic aspirants. When Innocent ii. came to France for support, Cluny sent sixty horses and mules to meet him, and entertained him and all his followers for eleven days. At an earlier date it had lodged pope, king, and emperor, with all their followers, without displacing a single monk. Yet with all its wealth and magnitude the abbey maintained a strict observance of the rule of St. Benedict. Peter was too cultured and human-istic[1] for the Cistercians, who often criticised the half-heartedness of his community. In point of fact a strict order and discipline were maintained in the abbey, and Abélard entered fervently into its life. From their beds of straw the monks would rise at midnight and proceed to the church, where they would chant their long, dirge-like matins, and remain in meditation until dawn. Work, study, and prayer filled up the long hours; and at night they would cast themselves down, just as they were, on the bags of straw, to rise again on the morrow for the same task. Such monks—they are rare now, though far from ex-tinct—must be men of one idea—heaven. To that stage had Abélard sunk.

Years afterwards the brothers used to point out to visitors—for Abélard had left a repute

---

[1] Amongst other humane modifications we may note that he raised the age of admission to the abbey to twenty-one.

for sanctity behind him—a great lime-tree under which he used to sit and read between exercises. Peter had gone so far as to make him prior of the studies of the brethren, so lightly did he hold the charge of heresy. The abbot has given us, in a later letter to Heloise, an enthusiastic picture, drawn from the purely Buddhist point of view, of Abélard's closing days. With a vague allusion to this letter certain ecclesiastical writers represent Abélard as a sinner up to the time of the Council of Sens, and a convert and penitent in the brief subsequent period. In point of fact there was little change in the soul of the fallen man, beyond a weary resignation of his hope of cleansing the Church, involving, as this did, a more constant preoccupation with the world to come. The abbot says, in support of his declaration, that Abélard had cast a radiance on their abbey, that 'not a moment passed but he was either praying or reading or writing or composing'; and again : 'If I mistake not I never saw his equal in lowliness of habit and conduct, so much so that Germain did not seem more humble nor Martin poorer than he to those who were of good discernment.' The 'good discernment' reminds us that we must not take at too literal a value this

letter of comfort to the widowed abbess. Abélard
had been an ascetic and a devout man since his
frightful experience at Paris twenty-five years previously. With the fading of his interest in the
things of earth, and in his sure consciousness of
approaching death, his prayers would assuredly
be longer and his indifference to comfort and
honour more pronounced.

But we have a clear indication that there was
no change in his thoughts, even in that last year,
with regard to the great work of his life and
the temper of his opponents. During the quiet
months of teaching at Cluny, a certain 'Dagobert
and his nephew' asked him for a copy of his
dialectical treatise, one of his earliest writings.
It is impossible to say whether this Dagobert was
his brother at Nantes (where Astrolabe also
seems to have lived) or a monastic 'Brother
Dagobert.' Most probably it was the former,
because he speaks of the effort it costs him, ill
and weary of writing as he is, to respond to their
'affection.' He does not copy, but rewrites his
dialectics, so that we have in the work his last
attitude on his studies and his struggles. It is
entirely unchanged. Jealousy, hatred, and ignorance are the sole sources of the hostility to his

work. They say he should have confined himself
to dialectics (as Otto von Freising said later); but
he points out that his enemies quarrelled even
with his exclusive attention to dialectics, firstly
because it had no direct relation to faith, and
secondly because it was indirectly destructive of
faith. He has still the old enthusiasm for reason
and for the deepening and widening of our natural
knowledge. Both knowledge and faith come
from God, and cannot contradict each other. It
was the last gleam of the dying light, but it was
wholly unchanged in its purity.

With the approach of spring the abbot sent the
doomed man to a more friendly and familiar
climate. Cluny had a priory outside the town
of Chalon-sur-Saône, not far from the bank of
the river. It was one of the most pleasant situations in Burgundy, in the mild valley of the Seine,
which Abélard had learned to love. But the
last struggle had exhausted his strength, and the
disease, variously described as a fever and a
disease of the skin, met with little resistance.
He died on the 21st of April 1142, in the sixty-
third year of his age.

How deeply he had impressed the monks of
St. Marcellus during his brief stay with them

becomes apparent in the later history, which recalls the last chapter in the lives of some of the most popular saints. It will be remembered that Abélard had, in one of his letters to Heloise, asked that his body might be buried at the Paraclete, 'for he knew no place that was safer or more salutary for a sorrowing soul.' Heloise informed the abbot of Cluny of the request, and he promised to see it fulfilled. But he found that the monks of St. Marcellus were violently opposed to the idea of robbing them of the poor body that had been hunted from end to end of France whilst the great mind yet dwelt in it. There have often been such quarrels, sometimes leading to bloodshed, over the bodies of the saints. However, the abbot found a means to steal the body from the monastery chapel in the month of November, and had it conveyed secretly, under his personal conduct, to the Paraclete.

We have a letter which was written by the abbot about this time to Heloise. I have already quoted the portion in which he consoles her with a picture of the edifying life and death of her husband. The first part of the letter is even more interesting in its testimony to the gifts and character of the abbess herself. Peter the Venerable was, it will be remembered, a noble of high origin, an abbot of great and honourable repute, a man of culture and sober judgment.

'For in truth,' he says, after an allusion to some gifts—probably altar-work—that she had sent him, 'my affection for thee is not of recent growth, but of long standing. I had hardly passed the bounds of youth, hardly come to man's estate, when the repute, if not yet of thy religious fervour, at least of thy becoming and praiseworthy studies, reached my ears. I remember hearing at that time of a woman who, though still involved in the toils of the world, devoted herself to letters and to the pursuit of wisdom, which is a rare occurrence. . . . In that pursuit thou hast not only excelled amongst women, but there are few men whom thou hast not surpassed.' He passes to the consideration of her religious 'vocation,' in which, of course, he discovers a rich blessing. 'These things, dearest sister in the Lord,' he concludes, 'I say by way of exhortation, not of flattery.' Then, after much theological and spiritual discussion, he says: 'It would be grateful to me to hold long converse with thee on these matters, because I not only take pleasure in thy renowned erudi-

tion, but I am even more attracted by that piety
of which so many speak to me.   Would that thou
didst dwell at Cluny !'

This is the one woman (and wife, to boot) to
whom Bernard could have referred in justification
of his equivocal remark to a stranger that Abélard
' busied himself with women.'   We have, however, little further record of the life of the
unfortunate Heloise.   Shortly after the body of
her husband has been buried in the crypt of their
convent-chapel, we find her applying to Peter of
Cluny for a written copy of the absolution of
Abélard.   The abbot sent it; and for long years
the ashes of the great master were guarded from
profanation by this pitiful certificate of his orthodoxy.   In the same letter Heloise thanks the
abbot for a promise that the abbey of Cluny will
chant the most solemn rites of the Church when
her own death is announced to them ; she also
asks Peter's favourable influence on behalf of
Astrolabe, her son, who has entered the service
of the Church.

Heloise survived her husband by twenty-one
years.   There is a pretty legend in the Chronicle
of the Church of Tours that the tomb of Abélard
was opened at her death and her remains laid in

it, and that the arms of the dead man opened wide to receive her whose embrace the hard world had denied him in life. It seems to have been at a later date that their ashes were really commingled. At the Revolution the Paraclete was secularised, and the remains of husband and wife began a series of removals in their great sarcophagus. In 1817 they found a fitting rest in Père Lachaise.

CHAPTER XV

THE INFLUENCE OF ABÉLARD

IF the inquirer into the influence of the famous
dialectician could content himself with merely
turning from the study of Abélard's opinions to
the towering structure of modern Catholic theology, he would be tempted to exclaim, in the
words of a familiar epitaph, 'Si monumentum
quaeris, circumspice.'   Abélard's most characteristic principles are now amongst the accepted
foundations of dogmatic theology ; most, or, at
all events, a large number, of the conclusions that
brought such wrath about him in the twelfth
century are now calmly taught in the schools of
Rome and Louvain and Freiburg.   Bernardism
has been almost banished from the courts of the
temple.   The modern theologian could not face
the modern world with the thoughts of the saint
whose bones are treasured in a thousand jewelled
reliquaries ; he must speak the thoughts of the

heretic, who lies by the side of his beloved, amidst the soldiers and statesmen, the actresses and courtesans, of Paris. The great political organisation that once found it expedient to patronise Bernardism has now taken the spirit of Abélard into the very heart of its official teaching.

There are few in England who will read such an assertion without a feeling of perplexity, if not incredulity. Far and wide over the realm of theology has the spirit of Abélard breathed ; and ever-widening spheres of Evangelicalism, Deism, Pantheism, and Agnosticism mark its growth. But it is understood that Rome has resisted the spirit of rationalism, and to-day, as ever, bids human reason bow in submission before the veiled mysteries of ' the deposit of revelation.'

Yet the assertion involves no strain or ingenuity of interpretation of Catholic theology. The notion that Rome rebukes the imperious claims of reason is one of a number of strangely-enduring fallacies concerning that Church. The truth of our thesis can be swiftly and clearly established. The one essential source of the antagonism of St. Bernard and Abélard was the question of the relations of faith and reason. ' Faith precedes intellect,' said the Cistercian ; ' Reason precedes faith,' said the

Benedictine. All other quarrels were secondary and were cognate to their profound and irreconcilable opposition on this point. M. Guizot adds a second fundamental opposition on the ethical side. This, however, was certainly of a secondary importance. Few historians hesitate to regard the famous struggle as being in the main a dispute over the rights and duties of reason.

Turn then from the pontificate of Innocent II. to that of Pius IX. and of Leo XIII. Towards the close of the last century, Huet, Bishop of Avranches, began to meet rationalistic attacks with a belittlement of human reason. The idea found favour with a class of apologists. De Bonald, Bonetty, Bautain, and others in France, and the Louvain theologians in Belgium, came entirely to repudiate the interference of reason with regard to higher truths, saying that their acceptance was solely a matter of faith and tradition. Well, the Church of Rome (to which all belonged) descended upon the new sect with a remarkable severity. Phrases that were purely Bernardist in form and substance were rigorously condemned. The French 'Traditionalists' were forced to subscribe to (amongst others) the following significant proposition : ' The use of reason precedes faith, and leads up to it, with the aid of revelation and grace.' It was the principle which Abélard's whole life was spent in vindicating. The Louvain men wriggled for many months under the heel of Rome. They were not suffered to rest until they had cast away the last diluted element of their theory.

The episode offers a very striking exhibition of the entire change of front of Rome with regard to 'the rights of reason.' There are many other official utterances in the same sense. An important provincial council, held at Cologne in 1860, and fully authorised, discussed the question at length. 'We have no faith,' it enacted, 'until we have seen with our reason that God is worthy of credence and that He has spoken to us'; and again, 'The firmness of faith . . . requires that he who believes must have a preliminary *rational certitude* of the existence of God and the fact of a revelation having come from Him, and he must have no prudent doubt on the matter.' In the Encyclical of 1846 even Pius ix. insisted on the same principle : 'Human reason, to avoid the danger of deception and error, must diligently search out the fact of a divine revelation, and must attain a *certainty* that the message comes from God, so that, as the Apostle most wisely ordains, it may offer Him a " reasonable service." ' The Vatican Council of 1870 was equally explicit. The modern Catholic theologian, in his treatise on faith, invariably defines it as an intellectual act, an acceptance of truths after a satisfactory rational inquiry into the authority that urges them. It is official Catholic teaching that faith is impossible without a previous rational certitude. Moreover, the theologian admits that every part and particle of the dogmatic system must meet the criticism of reason. In the positive sense it is indispensable that reason prove the existence of God, the authority of God, and the divinity of the Scriptures. In the negative sense, no single dogma must contain an assertion which is clearly opposed to a proved fact or to a clear pronouncement of human reason or the human conscience. These are not the speculations of advanced theologians, but the current teaching in the Roman schools and manuals [1] of dogmatic theology.

Thus has history vindicated the heretic. The multiplication of churches has made the Bernardist

[1] One of the most widely-used of these manuals at present is that of the learned Jesuit, Father Hurter. On p. 472 of the first volume one finds the Bernardist notions of faith sternly rejected, and variously attributed to 'Protestants,' 'Pietists,' and 'Kantists.'

notion of faith wholly untenable and unserviceable to Rome. Reason precedes faith ; reason must lead men to faith, and make faith acceptable to men. That is the gospel that now falls on the dead ear of the great master.

And when we pass from this fundamental principle or attitude to a consideration of special points of dogma we again meet with many a triumph. We have already seen how Abélard's ' novelties ' may be traced to a twofold criticism— ethical and intellectual—of the form in which Christian dogmas were accepted in his day. Without explicitly formulating it, Abélard proceeded on the principle which is now complacently laid down by the Catholic theologian, and was accepted by the Christian world at large a century or half a century ago : the principle that what is offered to us as revealed truth must be tested by the declarations of the mind and of the conscience. The intellectual criticism led him to alter the terms of the dogmas of the Trinity, the Incarnation, the Eucharist, and others ; the ethical criticism led him to modify the current theories of original sin, the atonement, penance, and so forth.

Now, even if we confine our attention to Roman theology, we find a large adoption of Abélard's singularly prophetic conclusions. As to the Trinity, it is now a universal and accepted practice to illustrate it by analogies derived from purely natural phenomena, which are always heretical if taken literally. One of the proudest achievements of St. Thomas and the schoolmen was the construction of an elaborate analogical conception of the Trinity. On the equally important question of Scripture Abélard's innovation proved prophetic. In that age of the doctrine of verbal inspiration he drew attention to the human element in the Bible. Even the Catholic Bible is no longer a monochrome. Abélard's speculation about the 'accidents' in the Eucharist—that they are based on the substance of the air—is now widely and freely accepted by theologians. His moral principles relating to sins done in ignorance and to 'suggestion, delectation, and consent'— both of which were condemned, at Bernard's demand—are recognised to be absolutely sound by the modern casuist. His notion of heaven is the current esoteric doctrine in Rome to-day; his theory of hell is widely held, in spite of a recent official censure ; his pleading for Plato and his fellow-heathens would be seconded by the average Catholic theologian of to-day.

It is hardly necessary to point out how entirely the non-Roman theology of the nineteenth century has accepted Abélard's spirit and conclusions. The broadest feature of the history of theology during the century has been the resumption and the development of the modifying process which was started by Abélard eight centuries ago. The world at large has taken up his speculations on the Incarnation, the atonement, original sin, responsibility, inspiration, confession, hell and heaven, and so many other points, and given them that development from which the dutiful son of the Church inconsistently shrank.[1] A curious and striking proof of this may be taken from Tholuck's dissertation on 'Abélard and Aquinas as interpreters of Scripture.' The dis-

[1] A typical illustration of the perplexity and inconsistency which resulted from the conflict of Abélard's critical moral sense with apparently fixed dogmas is seen in his treatment of original sin in the *Commentary on the Epistle to the Romans.* He finds two meanings for the word sin—guilt and punishment; and he strains his conscience to the point of admitting that we may inherit Adam's sin in the latter sense. Then comes the question of unbaptized children—whom Bernard calmly consigned to Hades—and he has to produce the extraordinary theory that the Divine Will is the standard of morality, and so cannot act unjustly. But his conscience asserts itself, and he goes on to say that their punishment will only be a negative one—the denial of the sight of God—and will only be inflicted on those children who, in the divine prescience, would have been wicked had they lived !

tinguished German theologian, who is the author of a well-known commentary on the Epistle to the Romans, says that when he read Abélard's commentary on that Epistle, in preparing his own work, he seriously hesitated whether it would not suffice to republish the forgotten work of Abélard instead of writing a new one. When one recollects what an epitome of theology such a commentary must be, one can appreciate not only the great homage it involves to the genius of the man whom Bernard scornfully calls a 'dabbler in theology,' but the extent to which Abélard anticipated the mature judgment of theological science.

It seems, however, a superfluous task to point out the acceptance of Abélard's spirit, method, and results by theology in general. The more interesting and important question is the acceptance of his ideas by the Church of Rome. That we have abundantly established, and we may now proceed to inquire whether, and to what extent, Abélard had a direct influence in the abandonment of the mystic attitude and the adoption of one which may be fairly entitled 'rationalistic.'

Here we have a much more difficult problem to deal with. It may at once be frankly avowed that there is little evidence of a direct transition of

Y

Abélard's ideas into the accepted scheme of theology. Some of the most careful and patient
biographers of Abélard, as a theologian, say that
we cannot claim for him any direct influence on
the course of theological development. Deutsch
points out that his works must have become rare,
and the few copies secretly preserved, after their
condemnation by the pope ; certainly few manuscripts of them have survived. He had formed
no theological school (as distinct from philosophical), or the beginning of one must have been
crushed at Sens. His Roman pupils and admirers
were probably not men who would cultivate
loyalty under unfavourable circumstances. The
schoolmen of the following century only know
Abélard from passages in Hugh of St. Victor and
others of his enemies. The first to reproduce
what Deutsch takes to be the characteristic spirit
or method of Abélard is Roger Bacon ; it is
extremely doubtful if he had any acquaintance
whatever with Abélard. The world was prepared
to receive the ideas of Abélard with some respect
in the thirteenth century, but it had then a task
which was too absorbing to allow a search for the
manuscripts of 'a certain Abélard,' as one later
theologian put it. The Arabians and Jews had

reintroduced Aristotle into Europe. He had come to stay ; and the schoolmen were engrossed in the work of fitting him with garments of Christian theology.

On the other hand there are historians, such as Reuter, who grant Abélard a large measure of direct influence on the development of theology. It is pointed out that a very large proportion of the masters of the next generation had studied under Abélard. Reuter instances Bernard Sylvester of Chartres and William of Conches, as well as Gilbert de la Porée. Clearer instances of direct influence are found in the case of Master Roland of Bologna (afterwards to ascend the papal throne under the name of Alexander III.) and Master Omnebene of the same city. It is, in any case, quite clear that Abélard was pre-eminently a teacher of teachers. On the other hand it would be incorrect to lay too much stress on the condemnation by Pope Innocent. All the world knew that Bernard had prudently kept the unexecuted Bull in his pocket, and that Abélard was teaching theology at Cluny, with the pope's approval, a few months after the condemnation.

It is best to distinguish once more between the spirit or method of Abélard and his particular critical conclusions. His conclusions, his suggestions for the reconstruction of certain dogmas, were lost to theological science. The cruder notions of the earlier age and of Bernard continued to be regarded as *the* truth for many centuries. Even the masters, such as Roland of Bologna, who did found their theology more conspicuously on that of Abélard, prudently deviated from his opinions where they were 'offensive to pious ears.' His treatment of the Trinity is, perhaps, an exception. Not that Abélard's favourite analogies—that of the seal and its impression, and so forth—were retained, but he had set an example in the rationalistic or naturalistic illustration of the mystery which persisted in the schools. All the great schoolmen of the following century accepted the Abélardist notion of a rationalistic illustration and defence of the Trinity. They constructed an elaborately meaningless analogy of it, and invented a 'virtual' distinction—a mental distinction which might be taken to be objective for apologetic purposes—between the essence and the personalities. But Abélard's penetrating and reconstructive criticisms of the current dogmas of original sin, the Incarnation, responsibility, reward and punishment, inspiration, omnipotence, etc., degenerated into, at the most, obscure heresies—sank back into the well of truth until long after a rebellious monk had broken the bonds which held the intellect of Europe.

It was far otherwise with the spirit of Abélard, the fundamental principle or maxim on which all else depended. The thirteenth century cordially accepted that principle, and applied itself to the rationalisation of theology. It wholly abandoned the mysticism of Bernard and the school of St. Victor. The Cistercian had summed up Abélard's misdeeds thus in his letter to the pope : ' He peers into the heavens and searches the hidden things of God, then, returning to us, he holds discourse on ineffable things of which a man may not speak.' In the very sense in which this was said of Abélard, it may be urged as a chief characteristic of the saintly schoolmen of the thirteenth century. Even St. Bonaventure was no mystic in the anti-rational sense of Bernard ; simply, he applied to theology the reason of Plato instead of the reason of Aristotle. Archbishop Roger Vaughan, in his *Life of St. Thomas*, says that the schoolmen owed the ' *probatur ratione* ' in their *loci theologici* to Abélard. That is already a most striking vindication of Abélard's characteristic teaching as to the function of reason, for we know how important the 'proofs from reason' were in the scheme of Aquinas and Scotus. But they really owe far more than this to Abélard. If they have deserted the dreamy, rambling, fruitless, and fantastic speculation of the mystic school for a methodical and syllogistic inquiry concerning each point of faith, it is largely due to the example of Abélard. The schoolmen notoriously followed Peter the Lombard. From the *Sentences* of Peter the Lombard to the *Sic et Non* of Peter Abélard— through such works as the *Sentences* of Roland and Omnebene of Bologna and the so-called *Sentences of Peter Abélard*—is a short and easy journey. No doubt we must not lose sight of that other event which so powerfully influenced the theology of the thirteenth century : the invasion of the Arab and Jew philosophers. Theirs is the only influence of which the schoolmen show any consciousness in their elaborate fortification of dogma to meet the criticism of reason and conscience—except for the avowed influence of the Lombard ; and along that line we may trace the direct influence of Abélard.

In the circumstances it makes little difference

to the prestige of Abélard whether we succeed in proving a direct influence or no. There are few who will think less of him because he was beaten by St. Bernard in diplomatic manipulation of the political force of the Church. The times were not ripe for the acceptance of his particular criticisms, and the mystic school was the natural expression of this conservatism. We may even doubt if Deutsch is correct in saying that the thirteenth century was prepared to receive them, but that its attention was diverted to Spain. Renan has said that they who study the thirteenth century closely are astonished that Protestantism did not arise three hundred years earlier. That is the point of view of a logician. The Reformation was not in reality, though it seems such in theory to the student of the history of ideas, an intellectual development. No doubt it could not have succeeded without this development to appeal to, but it was a moral and political revolt. How little the world was prepared for such a revolt at the end of the thirteenth century may be gathered from a study of the life of that other rebellious monk, William Occam. This success the Anselms and Bernards achieved: they spread, with a moral renovation, a spirit of docility and loyalty to the Church.   The subtlety and intellectual activity they could not arrest came to be used up in an effort to restate the older dogmas in terms which should be at once conservative and acceptable to the new rational demand.

It is equally difficult and more interesting to determine how far Abélard himself was created by predecessors.   Nowadays no thought is revolutionary ; but some notions are more rapid in their evolution than others.   To what extent Abélard's ideas were thus borrowed from previous thinkers it is not easy to determine with precision.   He was far from being the first rationalist of the Middle Ages.   Scotus Erigena and Bérenger (of anti-sacramental fame) were well remembered in his day.   He himself studied under a rationalistic master—Jean Roscelin, canon of Compiègne, —in his early years.   We do not know with certainty at what age he studied under Roscelin, and cannot, therefore, determine how great an influence the older master exercised over him. But there can be little doubt that Abélard must be credited with a very large force of original genius.   At the most, the attitude of his mind towards dogma was determined by outward influences, concurring with his own temperament and character of mind. It is more than probable that this attitude would have been adopted by him even had there been no predisposing influence whatever. His rationalism flows spontaneously and irresistibly from his type of mind and character. In the development of the rationalist principle we see the exclusive action of his own intelligence. To most of us in this generation such dogmatic reconstruction as Abélard urged seems obvious enough ; yet one needs little imagination to appreciate the mental power or, rather, penetration, which was necessary to realise its necessity in the twelfth century.

One is tempted at times to speculate on the probable development of Abélard's thoughts if that great shadow had not fallen on his life at so early a period. There are two Abélards. The older theologian, who is ever watchful to arrest his thoughts when they approach clear, fundamental dogmas, is not the natural development of the freethinking author of the *Sic et Non*. With the conversion to the ascetic ideal had come a greater awe in approaching truths which were implicitly accepted as divine. Yet we may well doubt if Abélard would ever have

z

advanced much beyond his actual limits. Starting from the world of ideas in which he lived, he would have needed an exceptional strength to proceed to any very defiant and revolutionary conclusions. He was not of the stuff of martyrs, of Scotus Erigena, or Arnold of Brescia. He had no particle of the political ability of Luther. But such as he is, gifted with a penetrating mind, and led by a humanist ideal that touched few of his contemporaries, pathetically irresolute and failing because the fates had made him the hero of a great drama and ironically denied him the hero's strength, he deserves at least to be drawn forth from the too deep shadow of a crude and unsympathetic tradition.

INDEX

347

Printed by T. and A. CONSTABLE, (late) Printers to Her Majesty
at the Edinburgh University Press